TRAVEL MAUI - BEAUTY, MAGIC, AND MIRACLES

A GUIDE TO THE NATURAL AND SPIRITUAL WONDERS OF MAUI, HAWAII

GREG SCHAEFER

CONTENTS

This book is dedicated to: Lahaina

And happy 80th birthdays Mom and Dad!

INTRODUCTION

Have you ever had one of those moments where the world seems to stop spinning just long enough for you to catch your breath and truly absorb the beauty around you? That was me, the first time I laid eyes on a pod of humpback whales, gently navigating the warm, cerulean waters of Maui. It was one of those 'hold your breath and stare' moments. As a fifty-year-old 'professional drifter' who's seen the sun set and rise on many horizons, I consider these kinds of moments a kind of religion. Maui, with its blend of pristine beaches, lush rainforests, and rugged volcanic peaks, tends to have that effect on people. It certainly did on me – enough to make me move there... twice!

As a wildlife biologist who's worked alongside the gentle beings of the ocean, I've developed a profound fascination with marine intelligence that we've only just begun to understand in whales, dolphins, octopi, and every last crazy critter beyond.

This book isn't your run-of-the-mill travel guide. It's a heartfelt invitation to explore Maui's natural wonders, those charted on maps and the hidden gems reserved for the curious and the respectful. It's about diving deep (sometimes quite literally) into the rich biodiversity that makes this island a bounty of ecological wonders. But more than that, it's about connecting with Maui on a spiritual and emotional level, allowing its magical landscapes and spirited wildlife to heal and inspire you, as they have done for me.

Through these pages, I aim to share not just a guide to the best snorkeling spots or the most breathtaking hikes but also tales of magical experiences and miraculous encounters that have moved the souls of many. I'll add local wisdom and cultural insights wherever possible, hoping to enrich your understanding of Maui.

Because I believe it's important to tread lightly and lovingly upon this earth, I'll share tips on exploring responsibly, in harmony with Maui's fragile ecosystems and vibrant communities.

So, whether you're planning your next adventure or simply daydreaming of tropical shores from the comfort of your home, consider this a personal invitation from a fellow drifter and dreamer. Let's ramble through Maui together, discovering its beauty, magic, and miracles.

FOREWORD - SOMEWHERE OVER THE RAINBOW

While I'm not usually the first to volunteer for such endeavors, I felt I was up for the task of supplying music for my sister Abbey's wedding, especially after she volunteered me for the job!

It wasn't going to be a burden on any level, as the music could only serve as background for what was destined to be a beautiful event on Napili Beach, Maui.

I had two primary tasks: securing a live musician for some pre/post ceremony and part of the reception and creating an iPod set list to fill in the rest of the festivities.

For the live musician, Abbey was interested in more of the standard acoustic guitar style sound and setlist. Most of the 'wedding singers' available for hire on Maui specialized in the infinitely-sentimental-but-not-necessarily-the-first-choice-for-an-entire-wedding-night traditional Hawaiian music sound, leaving my options limited. Three exactly, and the first two I called were not available that day. The third and last hope for a wedding singer, a kindly fellow named Dirks, seemed to be available but hesitant. Ultimately, after at one point strangely saying 'I think I'm ready' during a phone conversation, he accepted the gig. That statement gave me pause, but I shook it off and moved on and hoped for the best, as I was out of options anyway.

After a long and rainy week of rounding up the friends and relatives in West Maui, the big day arrived. Right on cue, the persistent rainclouds retreated to sea, and the sun shone a soul-singing shade of maroon. Dirks, the wedding singer, sang for the pre-ceremony and was lovely. Then, as the formal wedding ceremony began, it was my time to shine. The walk-in song was on the groom's (my brother-in-law Philip) iPod. Nailed it. Now, I had the entire length of the ceremony to cue up the walk-off song.

The 'walk-off song' was to be the version of 'Somewhere Over the Rainbow' by the late Hawaiian musician Israel Kamakawiwo'ole, also known as "Iz." If you know it, you know it, and if you don't, please add it to your setlist 'for a happier life.'

Then the proverbial sh*t started to hit the fan.

I went to Phillips iPod to cue up 'Somewhere Over the Rainbow,' and it wasn't there. Those early iPods were pretty simple. Search by song, singer or setlist. The song wasn't there anymore.

Thank goodness I had the same track on my iPod as well. So, I plugged in my iPod and went to cue up Iz's version of "Somewhere Over the Rainbow."

But it wasn't there, either.

Search by song, singer, or setlist, it wasn't there anymore.

It wasn't actually possible. If you remember, those first-generation iPods could only be modified (songs added or removed) by plugging in, via physical cord, to your computer and logging into your iTunes account. There was no option for adding or deleting songs wirelessly.

It wasn't possible that the song disappeared from either or BOTH iPods for that matter!

Now white-hot-panic is setting in, as my sister's wedding was about to end in awkward silence and thus single-handedly be ruined by me who had like one job...

Dirks was sitting right next to me and could see my panic setting in, so he asked me what was wrong.

I said the walk-off song has f'ing magically disappeared from both iPods.

He asked what song and I said: "Somewhere Over the Rainbow by Iz"

Dirks went silent.

I went back to frantically searching and re-searching both iPods, searching by song, artist, and setlist. Search again. It was just here this morning, and now it's gone, on both iPods.

Then I hear Dirks behind me say: 'I think I can do it.'

I paused but then politely said, 'No thanks' (he can't really hope to duplicate the Iz version that was my sister's choice for her freaking wedding walk-off song), and I returned to my frantic search.

As I continue futile, manic, systematic three searches on two iPods, I hear Dirks behind me start to practice the song's high notes very quietly.

I continued a panicked search; I heard him behind me say: 'I can sing it.'

I vaguely shake my head, but time is running out.

The bride and groom are kissing...

My hundred searches turned up empty...

I turn to Dirks and give him a green light via a helpless, hopeless shrug.

He sings a perfectly lovely version of Somewhere, Over the Rainbow as my sister Abbey and her new husband, Philip, walk into the stunningly picture-perfect Maui sunset.

From that moment, the festivities flowed into the reception, where Dirks sang for the first hour, and then I switched over to my iPod setlist for the duration. All systems go, no glitches. I wasn't going to ruin this part of the wedding day too.

Shortly into the reception, I apprehensively approached my new Brother-in-law Philip to ask if he noticed the walk-off song switcharoo/debacle. He curiously tipped his head but then admitted no, was lost in the ether of the moment. (My sister later said the same thing). He asked me why I had made the switch, and I explained that the music files had impossibly vanished from both iPods. I had both in my pocket and returned his. He looked perplexed as if that weren't possible. He clicked it on, searched by song, and it was right there. He showed me. It was exactly where it was supposed to be. I couldn't process this. I assumed I was losing my mind and decided it must be time for a Gin and Tonic.

While in line at the bar, I couldn't resist peeking at my own iPod again.

Search by song: 'Somewhere Over the Rainbow.'

It was right there where it was supposed to be.

Bartender, make it a double, please.

A couple of hours into the reception, the mood is Hawaiian bliss. I look across the room to see my sister conversing with Dirks, the singer. His back is to me, but my sister's very expressive face shows grave concern. While speaking with the new bride, Dirks has broken down in tears.

It eventually became clear why he muttered "I think I'm ready" in our first conversation several months ago.

It turns out, this was Dirks's first public singing gig in a year.

Two years prior, Dirks married the love of his life, Maria. Six months later, Maria was diagnosed with terminal cancer, and six months after that she was gone.

Maria, a deep lover of music, fell hopelessly in love with Dirks the very first moment she heard his voice sing out at a Sunday sunset gathering at Little Beach.

As she faced her last days, she wanted nothing more than to have Dirks singing to her at her bedside, which he did with every ounce of his soul.

In the very last hour, she requested her favorite song. He poured his heart out singing it, and then she said 'again'—and then again—and then she passed.

Indeed, the last song Dirks sang to Maria was: 'Somewhere Over the Rainbow.'

* * *

The previous tale about the events of my sister's wedding and the disappearing song is a true story with the names switched (for whatever reason that happens.)

You might be wondering how I will transition from that story to a 'travel guide'.

I'm not really sure; this is my first try at writing a book for crying out loud!

I guess if there's a segue for tragedy in beauty or beauty engulfed by tragedy... We might as well start with Lahaina.

LAHAINA

1.1 HISTORICAL MILESTONES

Lahaina, Maui, isn't just your typical beach town; it's a place where Hawaiian kings once roamed and whalers partied. Back in the day, before Maui became a hotspot for surfers and sunbathers, Lahaina was the capital of the Kingdom of Hawaii from 1820 to 1845. Imagine walking the same streets where King Kamehameha himself made big moves to unite the Hawaiian Islands.

This town wasn't just about royal affairs; it was a whaling hub in the mid-1800s. Sailors from around the globe dropped anchor in Lahaina to restock and revel after months at sea. The town was buzzing with taverns, and let's just say, things could get pretty wild. Fast forward, and the whaling era faded, but Lahaina found its next big thing: sugar plantations. This industry boom brought a mix of cultures to Maui, as workers from Asia and Europe came seeking jobs.

In modern times, Lahaina was more about stunning sunsets and cool art galleries than royal decisions and whaling tales. But stroll down Front Street, and you were walking through history. Places like the old Lahaina Courthouse and the massive Banyan Tree, planted in 1873, are reminders of the town's rich past.

And then, on one hot, dry, windy night in August, it was gone. Almost the entire town of Lahaina was burned to the ground…

1.2 UTTER DEVASTATION

On August 8, 2023, the historic town of Lahaina was engulfed by an unfathomable disaster. Fueled by extreme conditions, a wildfire swept through the area with devastating speed and intensity. The fire ravaged the heart of this beloved community, leaving in its wake a landscape of loss and desolation. Homes, landmarks, and centuries of history were consumed by flames, erasing lifetimes of memories in mere moments.

The residents of Lahaina, whose ancestors had navigated the vast Pacific to call this paradise home, found themselves facing an unimaginable reality. The fire not only claimed structures but also the very essence of community and belonging. The toll was heavy, with 100+ lives lost, and countless others forever altered by the tragedy.

In the aftermath, the world bore witness to the profound grief and resilience of Lahaina's people. The community, bound by a shared sorrow, began the slow healing process, clinging to hope amidst the ruins. The story of the 2023

Lahaina fire is a somber reminder of nature's unpredictable power and the fragility of human existence. It underscores the importance of unity and strength in facing adversity, as Lahaina looks toward a future of recovery and renewal.

1.3 LESSONS LEARNED

The fire taught Lahaina and its people invaluable lessons about preparedness, community strength, and the critical importance of preserving cultural heritage. It made clear the importance of community emergency plans and the value of regular drills, ensuring that Lahaina would be better prepared for any future challenges. The disaster also underscored the need for sustainable practices in both building and living areas to minimize environmental impacts and reduce the risk of future fires.

Perhaps the most enduring lesson, however, is the power of community. In the face of adversity, the people of Lahaina showed that unity, compassion, and resilience can overcome even the most daunting challenges. This lesson resonates beyond the shores of Maui, inspiring all who hear it to cherish and protect their own communities and cultural heritage for future generations.

The fire of 2023 will undoubtedly be remembered as the most pivotal moment in Lahaina's history. Yet, more than the destruction, it will be the stories of resilience, rebirth, and unwavering community spirit that will define this chapter. Lahaina stands not just as a place but as a symbol of hope and strength, a beacon for all who face their own fires, literal or metaphorical, reminding them that from the ashes, new beginnings can and will flourish.

Supporting Lahaina

The waves of support from people worldwide buoy the spirit of Lahaina. Visitors play a crucial role in the town's recovery, and numerous ways exist to contribute to its resurgence. One of the most impactful is simply by being there – patronizing local businesses, dining at local restaurants, and purchasing goods from local artisans. Each dollar spent in Maui helps fuel Lahaina's economy, supporting families and funding reconstruction efforts.

For those looking to leave a lasting impact, participating in community-led restoration projects offers a hands-on way to help. Beach clean-ups, restoration drives, and cultural preservation activities aid the town's physical rebuilding and strengthen the bonds between visitors and this remarkable community. It's an opportunity to experience the true essence of aloha, understanding that it's more than a greeting —it's a way of living, of giving, and of supporting each other.

1.4 THE BANYAN TREE

In the heart of Lahaina, standing with a presence so grand it seems to hold Maui's history in its branches, is the Banyan Tree. It was Planted in 1873 to honor of the 50th anniversary of the first Protestant mission in Lahaina. This tree has grown from a mere 8-foot sapling to a sprawling giant whose canopy covers an entire city block. It's not just a tree; it's a living monument, a witness to Lahaina's unfolding history.

Underneath its expansive shade, the Banyan Tree serves as Lahaina's communal heartbeat. This tree has been the backdrop to countless cultural gatherings, art fairs, and celebrations, turning it into a symbol of community and creativity. The tree's ability to bring people together to serve as a natural amphitheater for the stories and dreams of both kama'aina (locals) and malihini (visitors) underscores its importance beyond the physical.

But the Banyan Tree's significance extends into the ecological realm. As one of the largest of its kind in the United States, it plays a vital role in Lahaina's ecosystem. Its vast network of trunks and branches provides a sanctuary for birds and a cool respite from the relentless Lahaina sun, not just for humans but for countless species.

As of the time I am writing this, it has been eight months since the Lahaina fire and the Banyan tree has suffered significant injuries, but it is still alive. Numerous people and organizations are working to revive this magnificent tree. Efforts to maintain its health include regular check-ups by arborists, careful monitoring of its growth, and community education about its importance. It's a living lesson in environmental stewardship, showing how nature and culture can thrive together if cared for with respect and aloha.

However, what's more important is that this tree has left a lasting impression on the hearts and minds of the countless hundreds of thousands of people who have had the privilege of being in its presence. It is heartening to see so many people from around the world rooting for the recovery of a single tree, underscoring humans' profound need to remain truly connected to nature.

THE ALOHA SPIRIT AND KAPU -
MAUI'S HEARTBEAT

I magine stepping off the plane and being greeted by a warm breeze that whispers "welcome" with every gentle gust. That's the Aloha Spirit, an invisible embrace that wraps around you the moment you set foot on Maui. It's in the air, the sea, and the smiles of those you meet. This chapter explores the essence of Aloha, a deeply embedded concept in Hawaiian culture that shapes the island's soul.

2.1 UNDERSTANDING ALOHA

Aloha is the thread that weaves through the fabric of life in Hawaii, binding its people with a philosophy steeped in love, peace, and compassion. It's a greeting, a farewell, and a way of living that encourages us to genuinely care for others and our environment. More than just a word, Aloha is a lens through which Hawaiians view the world, a guide for interacting with kindness and empathy.

Historical Roots

Aloha's roots run deep, tracing back to the earliest Polynesian navigators who settled these islands. For centuries, it has been a cornerstone of Hawaiian culture, guiding social interactions and relationships. It reflects the island's history, from the times of ancient kapu (taboo) systems to the modern day, serving as a constant reminder of the importance of harmony and respect in the community.

Living Aloha

For visitors, embracing the Aloha Spirit can transform a simple vacation into a truly enriching experience. It starts with small gestures - a smile to a stranger, patience in line, or a heartfelt "mahalo" (thank you) to your server. But it goes beyond manners. Living Aloha means approaching Maui and its people with an open heart, ready to learn and appreciate the island's traditions and values. It's about making connections that last well beyond your stay, fostering a sense of kuleana (responsibility) to preserve and protect the beauty around you.

- **Morning Rituals**: Start your day with a moment of gratitude for the island's beauty. Whether it's a sunrise at Haleakala or the sound of waves from your balcony, acknowledging Maui's wonders sets the tone for a day lived in Aloha.
- **Interactions with Locals**: Genuinely engage with the people you meet. Listen to their stories, ask about their traditions, and share a bit of your own journey.

These interactions will add layers of meaning to your visit.

- **Environmental Respect**: Practice Aloha by respecting Maui's natural environment. Stick to marked trails when hiking, use reef-safe sunscreen, and participate in beach clean-ups if you have the opportunity.

Aloha as a Cultural Pillar

Aloha isn't just personal; it's institutional. It influences everything from daily interactions to state laws in Hawaii. For instance, the "Aloha Spirit Law" is an actual part of Hawaii's Revised Statutes. It encourages government officials to treat people with deep care and respect and reflect the values of Aloha in their work. This law is a testament to how integral the concept is, not just in guiding personal behavior but in shaping the governance and societal structure of the islands.

2.2 NAVIGATING THE SACRED: UNDERSTANDING KAPU

In the heart of Hawaii's cultural history lies an intricate system known as Kapu, a set of ancient codes that once dictated every aspect of Hawaiian life. Kapu, translating to "forbidden" or "sacred" in Hawaiian, encompassed a range of sacred laws, rules, and regulations that were integral to maintaining balance and order within society. This complex system, deeply rooted in the connection between the people, the land, and the divine, offers a glimpse into the spiritual and social foundations of ancient Hawaiian society.

Definition of Kapu

The Kapu system was a cornerstone of traditional Hawaiian culture, guiding daily activities, social interactions, and religious practices. It was more than just a list of dos and don'ts; it was a way of life, deeply intertwined with the concepts of mana (spiritual power) and pono (righteousness). Kapu governed everything from fishing seasons to farming techniques, ensuring that resources were used sustainably and that the sacred remained untouched by the profane.

Impact on Society

The influence of Kapu on ancient Hawaiian society was profound. It shaped the social structure, dictating the community's roles and responsibilities, and was central to the political and religious systems. Under Kapu, chiefs and priests wielded significant power, acting as intermediaries between the gods and the people. The system also enforced strict taboos around sacred places and persons, creating a tangible sense of reverence and respect for the divine in everyday life.

Kapu played a crucial role in conserving Hawaii's natural resources. The system effectively managed resource use by declaring certain areas or species as kapu during specific times, allowing for regeneration and sustainability. This deep understanding of ecological balance showcases the wisdom and foresight of ancient Hawaiian practices.

Kapu in Modern Times

Though the formal Kapu system was abolished in the early 19th century, its principles continue to resonate in Hawaii today. The modern concept of malama 'aina (caring for the land) echoes the sustainability practices mandated by Kapu. Sacred sites, though no longer under the strict protections of Kapu, are still treated with respect and reverence by Hawaiians and visitors alike.

For travelers to Maui, an understanding of Kapu can enrich their experience, providing a deeper appreciation for the island's cultural sites and natural beauty. Recognizing the sacredness of these places encourages a mindful approach to exploration, one that honors the spiritual and historical significance of the land.

Respecting Kapu

As visitors to Maui, it's crucial to approach the island's sacred sites and cultural practices with sensitivity and respect. While the Kapu system may no longer be in force, the spirit of reverence for the sacred remains a vital part of Hawaiian culture. Here are some guidelines to help travelers navigate these sacred spaces with care:

- **Research Before You Visit**: Take time to learn about the sites you plan to explore. Understanding their history and significance can deepen your appreciation and guide your behavior.
- **Observe Signage and Guidelines**: Many sacred sites have specific rules or requests for visitors, such as

not taking photographs or entering certain areas. Adhering to these guidelines shows respect for the site and its cultural importance.

- **Leave No Trace**: Treat every site with care and leave it as you found it. This practice aligns with Kapu's advocacy for the sustainable use of resources.
- **Engage with Humility and Openness**: Approach interactions with locals and cultural practitioners with a willingness to listen and learn. Their insights can offer invaluable perspectives on the significance of Kapu and its modern manifestations.

By respecting Kapu and the principles it embodies, visitors can forge a meaningful connection with Maui that goes beyond the island's surface beauty. This respectful approach ensures that the sacred spaces and practices that have sustained Hawaiian culture for centuries continue to be honored and preserved for future generations.

In the shadows of Maui's lush landscapes and within the whispers of the ocean breeze, Kapu's legacy gently guides residents and visitors toward harmonious coexistence with the land and each other. As you wander through the island's sacred sites, let Kapu's ancient wisdom inspire you to move through the world with respect, mindfulness, and an appreciation for the delicate balance that sustains us all.

THE HISTORY, GEOLOGY, AND LANGUAGE OF MAUI

3.1 A BRIEF HISTORY OF MAUI

Maui boasts a rich history that spans centuries, blending natural wonders with cultural heritage. Named after the demigod Māui, who according to legend, pulled the Hawaiian Islands from the sea with his magical fishhook, the island has been a crossroads of Polynesian culture and tradition since its initial settlement by Polynesians in around 450-800 AD. These early settlers arrived in double-hulled canoes, navigating vast distances using the stars, and established thriving communities based on fishing, taro cultivation, and the principles of 'ohana (family) and aloha (love, peace).

In the late 18th century, Maui became part of the unified Kingdom of Hawaii under King Kamehameha the Great, marking a significant era of political consolidation. The 19th century introduced dramatic changes with the arrival of Western missionaries and traders, leading to the growth of sugar cane and pineapple plantations, which profoundly shaped Maui's economy and landscape. The multicultural workforce brought to work these plantations from Japan, China, Portugal, and the Philippines added to the island's diverse culture.

Maui also played a crucial role during World War II, serving as a strategic location for training soldiers and sailors. The 20th century saw the decline of the plantation economy and the rise of tourism as Maui's primary industry, transforming the island into a world-renowned destination known for its breathtaking natural beauty, including the lush Hana rainforest, the majestic Haleakalā volcano, and the historic whaling town of Lahaina.

Maui has played a significant role in developing modern oceanic navigation techniques. The Hokule'a, a replica of an ancient Polynesian double-hulled voyaging canoe, was launched in the 1970s as part of the Hawaiian Renaissance, a cultural revival movement. It sailed from Hawaii to Tahiti without modern navigation instruments, thus reviving and celebrating traditional Polynesian navigational skills.

Today, Maui honors its past while looking toward the future. It preserves its natural landscapes and cultural heritage, making it not just a tourist destination but a living museum of Polynesian history and a testament to its people's resilience and spirit.

3.2 GEOLOGICAL MARVELS

Maui, known as the "Valley Isle," showcases a diverse and dynamic geological landscape shaped by millions of years of volcanic activity, erosion, and coral growth. The island is part of the Hawaiian Island chain, formed by the Pacific Plate moving over a stationary hotspot in the Earth's mantle. This process led to the emergence of Maui's two major volcanoes: Haleakalā in the east and the West Maui Mountains.

Haleakalā, a massive shield volcano that constitutes more than 75% of the island, last erupted around 1790 and is renowned for its summit crater, which spans more than 7 miles across and is over 2,600 feet deep. The West Maui Mountains, older and heavily eroded, feature jagged peaks and deep valleys, remnants of a shield volcano that has been sculpted by centuries of rainfall.

The isthmus connecting these two volcanic masses was formed by the accumulation of lava flows and erosional deposits, creating a fertile plain that supports much of the island's agriculture. Maui's coastlines are a mix of sandy beaches and rugged lava cliffs, with coral reefs offering vibrant underwater ecosystems. The dynamic geological forces continue to shape Maui, creating a landscape of stunning natural beauty and diversity that tells the story of the Earth's ongoing evolution.

3.3 THE LANGUAGE OF THE LAND: HAWAIIAN TERMS YOU SHOULD KNOW

Stepping onto Maui's shores brings an air of enchantment. The Hawaiian language is a melodious and meaningful medium that offers a deeper understanding of the island's soul. Knowing a few key Hawaiian phrases and terms can open doors to rich interactions and insights, making your time on Maui even more memorable.

Common Phrases

With its soft vowels and rolling consonants, Hawaiian is a joy to speak. Here are some phrases that will not only be useful but will also help you connect more authentically with people you meet:

- **Mahalo** – Thank you. A simple word that expresses gratitude and appreciation.
- **Aloha** – Hello, goodbye, love. A versatile term that encapsulates the spirit of the islands.
- **'Ohana** – Family, but not just in a blood-related sense. It includes close friends, community, and anyone else you hold dear.
- **Kai** – Sea or ocean. Given Maui's deep connection with the surrounding waters, this is a term you'll hear often.
- **Ono** – Delicious. Whether you're savoring a plate of fresh poke or a tropical fruit you've never tried, this is the word to express your culinary delight.

Place Names

Maui's place names are more than mere labels; they are a reflection of the island's geography, history, and mythology. Understanding the meaning behind these names can enhance your appreciation of the places you visit. For example:

- **Haleakalā** translates to "House of the Sun," a name that captures the awe-inspiring sunrises viewed from the volcano's summit.
- **Lahaina**, meaning "cruel sun," speaks to the town's warm, dry climate.
- **Hāna** is derived from the Hawaiian word for 'work' or 'labor,' reflecting the area's history as a thriving agricultural hub.

Language Revival

Once at risk of fading into obscurity, the Hawaiian language has experienced a remarkable revival. This resurgence is possible thanks to the resilience of Hawaiian culture and a critical movement for preserving and celebrating indigenous identity. Schools dedicated to teaching entirely in Hawaiian, known as Kula Kaiapuni, play a pivotal role in this revival, nurturing a new generation fluent in the language of their ancestors. This resurgence has been instrumental in reinvigorating traditional practices, chants, and dances that rely on the nuances of the Hawaiian language to convey their full meaning and power.

Language as a Connection

For visitors, attempting to speak Hawaiian, even just a few words, is an act of respect that does not go unnoticed. It shows an eagerness to genuinely engage with the island's culture and can lead to more meaningful exchanges with locals. Beyond practical communication, these efforts can deepen your connection to Maui, allowing you to fully experience its beauty and spirit. The language carries the essence of the island's past and present, its people, and their stories. By learning and using Hawaiian terms, you're not just a visitor; you're a participant in the ongoing story of Maui.

As your days on Maui unfold, let the language guide you to moments of discovery and understanding. Each term you learn is a key to unlocking deeper layers of the island's identity, offering glimpses into the heart of this magical place. From the simple joy of correctly pronouncing a place name to the warmth of a shared "mahalo," these linguistic connections weave your experiences into the broader tapestry of Maui's cultural heritage.

In embracing the Hawaiian language, even in small ways, you're stepping into a stream of tradition that flows deep and strong. You're honoring the past, engaging with the present, and contributing to the future of this beautiful culture. So, as you explore the stunning landscapes, immerse yourself in the traditions, and meet the people who call this island home, remember that the language you carry with you can open worlds of understanding and connection.

MAUI'S GEOGRAPHICAL WONDER

I magine standing atop a giant volcano, silent beneath the cloak of night, waiting for the sun to perform its daily miracle. You're not just on any giant, but Haleakalā, the "House of the Sun," a place where the world seems to begin anew with each sunrise. This isn't hyperbole; it's what thousands feel when they witness the dawn over 10,000 feet above sea level. Maui's geography isn't just about stunning views or unique ecosystems; it's a protagonist in the island's story, shaping its culture, spirituality, and day-to-day life. From the summit of Haleakalā to the shores that embrace the Pacific, the island's landscapes tell tales of creation, navigation, and preservation.

4.1 HALEAKALĀ: HOUSE OF THE SUN

Sunrise and Sunset

The ritual of greeting the sun as it breaks the horizon atop Haleakalā is more than a must-do for visitors; it's a profound experience. The anticipation builds from the early hours of the morning as you ascend the winding road to the summit, a pilgrimage of sorts in the dark. As the first rays of light pierce the sky, painting it in orange, pink, and purple hues, it's hard not to feel a connection to something greater. This daily spectacle is not just a feast for the eyes but nourishment for the soul, rooted in the spirituality and traditions of the island. Why do people wake up in the middle of the night to make this journey? Perhaps it's the promise of starting anew, of washing away yesterday's concerns with the first light of day.

Volcanic Landscape

Haleakalā's landscape is a stark reminder of the earth's power to create and destroy. The summit area, with its vast crater, looks more like a scene from Mars than Maui. Here, the ground beneath your feet tells the story of eruptions past, of lava flows that cooled in the open air, creating a terrain that challenges the notion of a tropical paradise. The surrounding biosphere is a study of survival, with plants and animals that have adapted to the harsh conditions. Exploring this landscape, you can't help but feel like a tiny speck in the grand timeline of the earth, a humbling and awe-inspiring realization.

Conservation Efforts

The importance of Haleakalā extends beyond its cultural and spiritual significance; it's also a critical habitat for endemic species found nowhere else on Earth. The Haleakalā National Park plays a crucial role in protecting this fragile ecosystem, balancing the needs of the native plants and animals with the desires of the thousands who visit each year. Efforts to preserve the area include controlling invasive species, restoring native habitats, and educating visitors about the importance of minimal-impact practices. When you visit, you're not just a tourist but a temporary guardian of this unique environment. Your actions, from staying on designated trails to packing out what you pack in, contribute to the conservation of this incredible place.

4.2 FROM SEA TO SUMMIT: MAUI'S UNIQUE BIOGEOGRAPHY

Maui's landscape is a living museum showcasing nature's artistry in creating diverse ecosystems, from dynamic coral reefs to silent, misty forests atop ancient volcanoes. The island's isolation in the middle of the Pacific Ocean has acted as a crucible for ecological development, leading to a world where each valley, each shoreline, and each mountaintop tells a story of evolution and survival.

Island Formation

The birth of Maui is a tale of fire, sculpted by the relentless forces beneath the Earth's crust. Volcanic eruptions on the ocean floor, occurring millions of years ago, piled lava high above the sea layer upon layer until the emerging land broke the water's surface. Over eons, erosion and the growth of coral reefs shaped the island, giving rise to the valleys, mountains, and coastlines that define Maui today.

Diverse Ecosystems

The journey from Maui's coastlines to its highest peaks passes through a dramatic variety of ecosystems, each distinct in character and life forms.

- **Coastal Ecosystems**: At sea level, the coral reefs are bustling cities of marine life, while the beaches—some with black sand formed from volcanic rock, others golden—serve as nesting grounds for sea turtles and resting spots for monk seals.
- **Lowland Forests**: Moving inland, the lowland forests are alive with the chatter of birds and the rustle of leaves. They are home to various plants and animals that thrive in warm, damp conditions.
- **Montane and Subalpine Regions**: As elevation increases, the lush greenery gives way to the montane and subalpine regions of Haleakalā, where the air is cooler, and the vegetation becomes sparse. Here, the Silversword plant, with its silver leaves and towering bloom, is a rare gem, perfectly adapted to its harsh environment.
- **Alpine Summit**: At the highest elevations, the alpine summit area presents a landscape more akin to Mars than Maui, where only the hardiest life forms can survive.

This gradient of ecosystems from sea to summit illustrates the island's ecological diversity and underscores the intricate balance that sustains life in each unique environment.

4.3 READING THE CLOUDS: WEATHER PATTERNS AND TRAVEL PLANNING

With its lush landscapes and balmy beaches, Maui seems to live in perpetual summer. Yet the island's weather is a complex collection of microclimates, created by forces that create a range of climates within a small space. This diversity, while enchanting, plays a critical role in shaping your experience. So, let's navigate through the nuances of Maui's weather, ensuring your visit syncs perfectly with your adventure wish list.

Microclimates

Tucked within Maui's valleys, atop its volcanic peaks, and along its coastlines are microclimates, small but significant variations in weather that can change from sun to rain in just a few miles. These microclimates arise from the island's topography, with towering volcanoes and varied elevations creating pockets of climate that range from arid deserts to rain-soaked forests.

- **Haleakalā's Shadow**: The towering Haleakalā volcano casts a rain shadow over South Maui, creating areas with some of the lowest rainfall on the island. This phenomenon explains the arid landscapes of Kihei and Wailea, contrasting sharply with the lushness just a short drive away. Annual rainfall totals in the western Wailea might only reach 10 inches, while just 30 miles to the east rainfall totals can exceed 300 inches!

- **Windward and Leeward**: The northeastern, or windward, side of Maui welcomes the moisture-laden trade winds, which result in lush, green landscapes. In contrast, the southwestern, or leeward side, enjoys a drier, sunnier climate, perfect for beachgoers.

Understanding these microclimates is key to packing appropriately and selecting accommodations. If you're after sunny beach days, the leeward coasts are your best bet. But if you relish the thought of waking to misty mornings and exploring rainforests, the windward side calls.

Weather Phenomena

- **Trade Winds**: These prevailing winds, blowing from the northeast, are the architects of Maui's climate. They cool the air and bring moisture to the windward side. They're also a boon for sailors and windsurfers, offering ideal conditions for their pursuits.
- **Mauka Showers**: These "mountain showers" often occur in the late afternoon when warm air rises up the mountainsides, cools, and then precipitates. While these showers are usually brief, they're a magical spectacle, often leaving rainbows in their wake.

These phenomena shape the island's weather and daily rhythms. Planning activities around them, like hitting the beach in the morning when the trade winds are gentler, can enhance your experience.

Best Times to Visit

Choosing when to visit Maui hinges on what you're looking to experience. Here's a seasonal breakdown:

- **Winter (November to March)**: This is prime time for whale watchers, as humpback whales make their annual visit. Surfers also flock to the island, chasing the big winter waves. Do note that this is also the wettest season, especially on the windward side.
- **Spring (April to June)**: A sweet spot for visitors, spring offers a balance of sunny days and minimal rain. The island blooms in vibrant colors, and there are fewer crowds before the summer rush.
- **Summer (July to September)**: Expect warm, sunny days, especially in the leeward areas. During this season, the ocean is at its calmest, making it perfect for snorkeling, diving, and enjoying the beaches.
- **Fall (October to November)**: Similar to spring, fall offers a lull in tourist traffic and pleasant weather, though rainfall increases slightly as the season progresses.

Your activities can guide your decision. If snorkeling and diving are priorities, summer's calm seas are ideal. For hiking and exploring the island's interior, spring and fall's cooler temperatures and fewer rain showers create perfect conditions.

4.4 THE LUSH AND THE LAVA: MAUI'S DUAL LANDSCAPES

Contrasting Landscapes

Venture into the heart of Maui's rainforests, and you're enveloped in a world of perpetual green, where waterfalls cascade into crystal-clear pools and the air is heavy with the scent of wild ginger. These lush landscapes are the lungs of the island, a place where the cycle of life unfolds with an almost palpable intensity. Yet, not far from this explosion of life lie the volcanic badlands, areas where the earth has been sculpted by fire and time into landscapes that whisper of the planet's fiery heart. Here, the horizon stretches uninterrupted, and the stark beauty is as mesmerizing as it is desolate.

Adaptation and Survival

The flora and fauna of Maui have stories of adaptation that border on the miraculous. In the thriving rainforests, species have carved niches in the dense canopy and fertile ground, evolving in ways that intertwine them with the fabric of the forest. Contrastingly, the volcanic landscapes showcase life's tenacity; plants and animals here have developed ingenious survival strategies, from the Silversword's silver-hued leaves that reflect the sun's harsh rays to the 'Ōhi'a Lehua's ability to take root in solid lava.

Geological Activity

The forces that shaped Maui's landscapes are not relics of the past but ongoing processes that continue to mold the island. The volcanic areas are vivid reminders of the earth's restlessness. While Haleakalā has slumbered for centuries, its form clearly signals that the story of Maui's creation is far from over. Scientists monitor these sleeping giants closely, ensuring that any whispers of awakening are heard early.

THE MAJESTY OF MARINE WILDLIFE

5.1 WHALES (KOHOLĀ)

Maui is home to some of the ocean's most awe-inspiring inhabitants: whales. The relatively warm, calm waters between Maui, Moloka'i, and Lanai lure these gentle giants here, especially during the winter months. Curious about getting to know these majestic creatures a little better? Let's look at some of the most common whale species you might encounter near Maui.

- **Humpback Whales:** The superstars of Maui's whale-watching scene, humpback whales are as impressive as they are beloved. Let's stop here with the Humpbacks, as they deserve their own book section, which is coming soon!
- **False Killer Whales:** Despite their menacing name, false killer whales are large dolphins, reaching up to 20 feet long. They're known for their sociable nature,

often seen sharing food and forming strong bonds within their pods. These creatures have a playful side and occasionally interact with humans in the water. Though not as frequently spotted as humpbacks, they're a remarkable sight for those lucky enough to encounter them.

- **Pilot Whales:** Pilot whales, also part of the dolphin family, come in two varieties. Around Maui, you're likely to see the short-finned type. They can grow up to 24 feet in length and are notable for their deep dives in search of squid, their preferred snack. Living in large, complex social structures, these animals showcase the importance of family and community in the cetacean world.

And a few that are rare to see but it's good to dream:

- **Sperm Whales:** The largest of the toothed whales, sperm whales are a rare but awe-inspiring sight. Males can reach lengths of up to 60 feet, with their massive heads making up one-third of their body length. They are known for their incredible dives, plunging over 2,000 meters deep and holding their breath for up to 90 minutes to hunt squid. Sperm whales have a complex social structure and communicate using a series of clicks, which are among the loudest sounds in the animal kingdom.
- **Minke Whales:** Minke whales might be the smallest of the baleen whales found near Maui, but what they lack in size, they make up for in curiosity. Growing up to 30 feet long, these whales are known for their

inquisitive nature, often approaching boats and divers. While they're not as commonly observed as the humpbacks, a close encounter with a minke whale is an unforgettable experience, marked by their graceful movements and sleek appearance.

- **Blue Whales:** Though sightings are incredibly rare, blue whales – the largest animals ever known to have lived on Earth – occasionally pass through Hawaiian waters. These leviathans can reach lengths of up to 100 feet and weigh as much as 200 tons. Their sheer size is mind-boggling, with hearts the size of a small car and tongues weighing as much as an elephant. Spotting a blue whale is a once-in-a-lifetime event that underscores the breathtaking diversity and scale of marine life near Maui.

5.2 THE MAGNIFICENT HUMPBACK WHALE

Size and Splendor

Humpback whales, scientifically known as Megaptera novaeangliae, are true behemoths of the ocean. Picture a creature stretching 40 to 50 feet in length and weighing a staggering 30 to 40 tons. In the world of marine giants, humpbacks are the undisputed heavyweights. The sheer spectacle of witnessing these colossal beings, literally the size of a school bus, breach the surface is a memory you will cherish for life.

Beyond their sheer size, humpback whales exhibit remarkable intelligence and social complexity. Maui's waters become a stage for acrobatic displays – breaches, tail slaps, and pectoral fin waves that showcase their agility and communication skills. These behaviors are not mere performances; they are the language of the deep, a display of gestures that speak of bonds, hierarchy, and community.

Whale Migration Patterns

As winter descends on the northern seas, 10,000+ humpbacks gather in the sheltered waters of Maui to mate and give birth. The protected bays become maternity wards where newborn calves take their first breaths and learn the art of survival from their watchful mothers. Witnessing this delicate display of new life amidst the vastness of the Pacific is truly a gift to anyone who happens to grace their presence.

This annual migration kicks off in late fall, with the whales leaving the chilly Alaskan waters and traveling 3000 miles in search of Hawaii's tropical embrace. The peak of this visit falls between January and March, a period when the ocean near Maui becomes a stage for one of nature's most spectacular performances!

Whale Behavior

Understanding the behavior and communication methods of humpback whales can deeply enrich your whale-watching experience. These creatures are known for their complex songs, a form of communication that can be heard for miles underwater. Males are the primary singers, using their melodies to attract mates or assert dominance. What makes these songs even more fascinating is their evolutionary nature. Over the years, the melodies undergo subtle changes, a cultural shift in the underwater realm. Scientists study these evolving tunes to unlock the secrets of humpback whale communication and unravel the mysteries hidden within the vastness of the Pacific.

Scientists have marveled at humpbacks' collaborative feeding techniques, where individuals work together to corral and capture prey. The ocean becomes their playground, a realm of intelligence where playfulness intertwines with purpose. Observing these gentle giants engage in complex behaviors reveals the depth of their social connections and the intricacies of their underwater lives.

Whale watching in Maui isn't just an item to tick off a travel bucket list; it's a chance to witness the spectacle of nature and connect with creatures that remind us of the ocean's depth and mystery. By approaching this experience with respect and curiosity, we ensure the safety and well-being of the humpback whales and enrich our understanding of the marine world and our place within it. So, as you scan the horizon for that telltale spray of water (blow) or the shadow of a giant beneath the waves, remember that you're part of a moment much bigger than a photograph or a memory. It's a moment of connection, of understanding, and, ultimately, of conservation.

Whale Watching Ethics

Watching a humpback whale breach the ocean's surface is an unforgettable experience, but it's vital to remember that we're guests in their home. Here are some guidelines to ensure that our curiosity doesn't disturb these magnificent creatures:

- Keep your distance. Regulations require boats to stay at least 100 yards away from the whales. If you're observing from a smaller vessel or kayak, this rule is even more crucial.
- Choose responsible tour operators who adhere to these guidelines and prioritize the whales' well-being over an up-close encounter.

Conservation Efforts

The humpback whale, once hunted to the brink of extinction, has made a remarkable comeback, thanks in part to global conservation efforts. In Maui, organizations like the Hawaiian Islands Humpback Whale National Marine Sanctuary work tirelessly to protect these creatures and their habitat. Visitors can support these efforts by:

- Participating in citizen science projects that help track whale populations and behaviors.
- Supporting local conservation groups through donations or by attending educational programs.

Whale Sanctuary

The Hawaiian Islands Humpback Whale National Marine Sanctuary plays a pivotal role in safeguarding these magnificent beings. Established as a safe haven, this sanctuary spans the waters where humpbacks congregate, mate, and nurture their young. It's a critical effort to protect a species that, despite rebounding from the brink of extinction, still faces threats from entanglement, collision with vessels, and environmental changes. The sanctuary is not just a protective boundary but a commitment to preserving and understanding humpback whales and their habitat.

Research and Monitoring

Dedicated scientists and volunteers anchor the heart of the sanctuary's mission. Through meticulous research and monitoring, they peel back the layers of mystery surrounding humpback whale behaviors and health. Tagging and tracking projects reveal migration patterns and habitat use, while photo identification helps estimate population sizes and monitor the health of individual whales. These efforts are crucial for the whales' protection and understanding how environmental changes affect them.

- **Genetic Studies**: Researchers collect skin samples to study genetics, which offers insights into whale breeding patterns and population dynamics.
- **Acoustic Monitoring**: Listening devices placed in the water capture the whales' songs and calls, aiding in studying their complex communication and its role in social structures.

Regulations for Whales

Navigating the balance between human activity and wildlife conservation led to establishing specific regulations and guidelines. These rules, enforced within the sanctuary, are designed to minimize human impact on the whales. Vessels must maintain a minimum distance from the whales, ensuring that these sensitive creatures are not disturbed during their critical breeding and nursing periods. Speed restrictions in whale-dense areas reduce the risk of collisions, protecting both the whales and boaters. By adhering to these guidelines, visitors and locals contribute to the safe coexistence with these oceanic giants.

Eco-conscious Whale Watching

Opting for eco-conscious whale-watching tours is a direct way to support conservation efforts. Operators committed to sustainability go beyond merely following regulations; they educate passengers about humpback whales and the importance of preserving their environment. On these tours, guests learn not just to observe but to appreciate and understand the significance of these whales within the ocean's ecosystem.

- **Small Group Tours**: Choosing tours that limit passenger numbers ensures a more intimate experience with minimal disturbance to the whales.
- **Educational Component**: Look for tours that offer educational insights, turning a simple outing into a learning opportunity about marine conservation.
- **Conservation Support**: Some tour operators contribute a portion of their proceeds to whale research and conservation projects. Opting for these tours helps fund ongoing efforts to protect humpback whales.

When it comes to whale watching on Maui, several companies stand out for their exceptional services, knowledgeable guides, and commitment to conservation. These tours offer a chance to witness the majestic humpback whales in their natural habitat, an experience that's both thrilling and educational.

- **Pacific Whale Foundation** – Renowned for its research and conservation efforts, Pacific Whale Foundation offers eco-friendly whale watching tours led by marine biologists, providing insightful commentary on whale behavior and conservation.
- **Maui Whale Watching Tours** – Praised for their smaller, intimate group sizes and personalized experiences, Maui Whale Watching Tours ensures close-up encounters with the whales, offering both morning and afternoon departures.
- **Trilogy Excursions** – Offering luxury sailing catamarans, Trilogy Excursions combines comfort with the excitement of whale watching. Their knowledgeable crew adds value with detailed explanations of the marine ecosystem.
- **Captain Steve's Rafting Adventures** – For an adventurous approach, Captain Steve's uses smaller, nimble rafts to get you closer to the whales, making for a thrilling and unforgettable experience.
- **Ultimate Whale Watch & Snorkel** – Specializing in small group tours, Ultimate Whale Watch & Snorkel provides a unique opportunity to observe whales up close, with a strong emphasis on respectful wildlife interactions and education.

Each of these companies offers a unique way to experience Maui's whale watching season, emphasizing respect for the marine environment and providing educational insights that make the experience all the more rewarding.

5.3 THE INTELLIGENT MANTA: ENCOUNTERS IN THE MOONLIGHT

A "Hahalua" is the Hawaiian term for the manta ray, a large species of ray. Characterized by their enormous size, manta rays can span up to 29 feet across, though the average is about 22 feet making it one of the largest fish in the ocean. These majestic beings belong to the family Mobulidae and are closely related to sharks. Their distinctive body shape sets them apart: a broad, flat body with triangular pectoral fins resembling wings that allow them to glide through the water with ease. These gentle giants are filter feeders, consuming large quantities of plankton which they funnel into their mouths as they swim.

In Hawaiian culture, the hahalua is highly respected and often considered an ʻaumākua, or guardian spirit, by some families. The manta ray symbolizes grace, elegance, and protection. Sightings of hahalua are thought to bring good luck, and they are revered for their peaceful nature and the majestic presence they command in the waters around the Hawaiian Islands. The cultural significance of the manta ray in Hawaii reflects the deep connection and respect the Hawaiian people have for the ocean and its inhabitants.

Despite their size, manta rays pose no threat to humans; they lack the stinging spine common to other rays.

Manta rays are also known for their intelligence and curiosity. They have the largest brain of all fish, which supports complex navigation, problem-solving, and social interactions. They've been observed engaging with divers and snorkelers, often approaching closely, showcasing a remarkable level of curiosity and playfulness.

Manta Ray Night Dives

These night dives present a scene straight from a dream, where divers and snorkelers float in the water, lights in hand, while manta rays sweep and soar below, funneling plankton into their open mouths. This feeding dance, a nightly ritual, showcases the manta's incredible adaptability and grace. Observing from a respectful distance, humans can watch as these gentle giants barrel roll and glide through the beams of light, creating a spectacle that's as mesmerizing as it is unforgettable. In these moments, suspended in the water's embrace, one can truly appreciate the complexity and beauty of marine life.

Conservation Status

Behind the awe-inspiring encounters with manta rays lies a story of vulnerability. Despite their size and strength, Mantas face numerous threats in the wild. Overfishing, habitat loss, and entanglement in fishing gear have led to a decline in their populations, prompting conservation groups to sound the alarm. Classified as vulnerable by the International Union for Conservation of Nature (IUCN), manta rays need our help to survive. Efforts to protect them range from establishing marine protected areas, enforcing sustainable fishing practices, and conducting research to better understand their needs and behaviors.

Manta Ray Mysteries

With their wide, wing-like fins and intelligent eyes, Manta rays are among the ocean's most fascinating inhabitants. Recent studies have shed light on their complex social behaviors, impressive navigation abilities, and even their capacity for problem-solving, hinting at a level of intelligence that rivals some land mammals. Mantas recognize themselves in mirrors, a trait indicative of self-awareness, and exhibit curiosity, often approaching divers to investigate. Their brain-to-body size ratio, one of the largest among fish, supports the notion that mantas are majestic and mindful creatures capable of complex thought and emotion.

As the night wears on and the dance of the mantas continues, those fortunate enough to witness it carry away more than just memories. They carry a sense of wonder, a deeper respect for the ocean and its inhabitants, and a reminder of the delicate balance that sustains all life on this planet. The encounter with manta rays under the moonlight becomes more than an adventure; it's an invitation to ponder, learn, and engage with the natural world in a way that honors its mysteries and its majesty.

5.4 DOLPHIN DELIGHT

In the waters surrounding Maui, two of the ocean's most beloved inhabitants play a significant role in the marine ecosystem and the island's cultural diversity. Dolphins, with their playful antics and serene grace, capture the hearts and minds of those lucky enough to encounter them!

Dolphin Species

Around Maui, you'll find three fantastic dolphin species that often capture the hearts of locals and visitors alike. First up, the **Spinner Dolphin**, famous for its acrobatic spins above the water. These playful creatures can launch themselves into the air and rotate several times before splashing back down, putting on a real show. It's believed they do this to shake off parasites or just for fun!

Next, we have the **Bottlenose Dolphin**, the dolphin celebrities of the world. You might recognize them from TV or movies thanks to their charismatic nature and intelligence. Bottlenose dolphins are known for their sociable behavior and often interact with humans in wild or captive settings. They have impressive problem-solving skills and a complex form of communication, making them fascinating to researchers and enthusiasts alike.

Then there's the **Pacific Spotted Dolphin**, which sports a distinctive spotted pattern as it matures. These dolphins are incredibly social and often seen in large groups, sometimes mingling with other dolphin species. They're known for their playful nature, often riding the bow waves of boats, much to the delight of onlookers.

Finally, a rare but thrilling sight to those lucky enough...

The **Orca,** or killer whale, is a highly intelligent, apex predator found in oceans worldwide, recognized by its distinctive black-and-white coloring. Adult males can reach up to 26 feet in length and weigh as much as 6 tons, making them the largest members of the dolphin family. Orcas are incredibly social creatures, living in complex, matriarchal societies with unique dialects, an example of their sophisticated communication abilities. Their intelligence is evident in their strategic hunting techniques, utilizing teamwork to capture prey ranging from fish to seals. Orcas have been known to exhibit behaviors such as teaching, learning, cooperation, and even grieving, highlighting their complex emotional and social intelligence.

Dolphin Intelligence and Empathy

Dolphins are marine marvels that showcase intelligence, social complexity, and, yes, even empathy. When we dive into the world of dolphins, we're not just talking about creatures who can follow simple commands or perform tricks for a fishy treat. We're venturing into the realm of sentient beings who exhibit behaviors and emotional capacities that can make us rethink the boundaries of animal intelligence.

First, dolphins have brains that are not only large for their body size—a trait associated with higher intelligence—but also intricately structured. This allows them to engage in behaviors that are the hallmarks of smarts: problem-solving, self-recognition, understanding abstract concepts, and even using tools. For instance, some dolphins use marine sponges to protect their snouts while foraging on the seafloor, a nifty trick passed down from generation to generation, showcasing tool use and cultural transmission of knowledge.

But dolphins' brainpower is not the only impressive feature; their emotional intelligence, particularly their capacity for empathy, truly sets them apart. Dolphins have been observed displaying behaviors that suggest a deep understanding of and care for the emotional states of others, both within their own species and beyond.

Take, for example, dolphins' interactions with each other and humans. Numerous accounts exist of dolphins coming to the aid of distressed swimmers, protecting them from sharks, or guiding them to safety. Such actions hint at an understanding of others' distress and a willingness to help, regardless of species—a hallmark of empathy.

Moreover, dolphins form incredibly strong social bonds within their pods and have been seen supporting sick or injured members, staying by their side, and helping them to the surface to breathe if needed. This behavior is not merely instinctual but reflects a conscious choice to help, driven by an understanding of the other's plight.

One of the most touching displays of dolphin empathy is their response to the death of a pod member. Dolphins exhibit what can only be described as mourning behavior, circling the deceased, gently nudging them, and even making vocalizations that suggest distress. These actions suggest a depth of emotional experience and social bonding that mirrors human expressions of grief and empathy.

Researchers studying dolphin behavior continue to uncover evidence of their sophisticated social structures and emotional lives, challenging our understanding of non-human intelligence and empathy. The stories and studies of dolphin intelligence and empathy fascinate us and invite us to consider the rich emotional lives of the animals with whom we share this planet.

Dolphins vividly remind us of the complexity and depth of animal intelligence and emotional capacity. Their empathy-driven actions extend a fin of friendship across the species barrier, urging us to recognize the value and richness of life in all its forms. As we continue to explore the depths of dolphin intelligence and empathy, we may find that these remarkable creatures have much to teach us about kindness, community, and the interconnectedness of all living beings.

ENDLESS UNDERWATER WONDERS - SNORKELING IN MAUI

M aui boasts some of the world's most stunning coral reefs and diverse marine ecosystems.

The coral ecosystems around Maui are crucial for marine biodiversity. They provide shelter, food, and breeding grounds for countless marine species, acting as the foundation for the ocean's food chain. These living structures, built over thousands of years by tiny coral polyps, are not just beautiful; they're vital to the health of the ocean and the planet. Snorkeling among the reefs, you're not just a visitor but a witness to the delicate balance that sustains life beneath the waves.

Identifying the fish that call these reefs home adds layers of excitement and appreciation to your snorkeling adventures. The variety is staggering from the iridescent parrotfish, whose grazing helps keep the coral clean, to the elusive moray eel, peeking out from its rocky hideaway. Here are a few tips to help you spot and identify these underwater residents:

- **Look for color patterns**: Many reef fish have distinctive color patterns that help with identification. The yellow tang, for example, is bright yellow all over, making it easy to spot against the blue ocean.
- **Observe behavior**: Some fish, like the pufferfish, are solitary, while others, like the convict tang, move in schools. Watching how fish behave can give you clues about their species.
- **Use a reference guide**: A waterproof fish identification card or guidebook can be a handy tool for snorkelers. These guides often include pictures and information about the most common species you're likely to encounter.

6.1 GREAT SNORKELING SPOTS OFF MAUI

Before we plunge into the marine wonderland, let's chart our course to some of the best snorkeling spots on the island. Maui offers a plethora of options, each with its unique charm.

- **Molokini Crater:** A crescent-shaped volcanic crater just off Maui's southwestern coast, Molokini is a marine sanctuary bursting with marine life. Clear waters and excellent visibility make this a prime spot for beginners and experienced snorkelers.
- **Ahihi Kinau Natural Area Reserve:** This reserve on Maui's southern coast offers a captivating mix of lava formations and coral gardens. With calm waters and abundant marine life, It is a fantastic destination for those seeking tranquility beneath the waves.

- **Honolua Bay:** Nestled on the northwest coast, Honolua Bay is a marine reserve boasting pristine coral reefs and an array of marine species. The bay is part of the larger Honolua-Mokuleia Bay Marine Life Conservation District, ensuring its protection for future generations.
- **Olowalu Reef:** This extensive coral reef along Maui's western coast is a haven for snorkelers. The shallow waters teem with colorful marine life, and the chance to encounter sea turtles makes Olowalu Reef a must-visit location.
- **La Perouse Bay:** At the southern end of Maui, near Ahihi Kinau, lies La Perouse Bay. The rugged lava landscape seamlessly transitions into crystal-clear waters, offering a unique snorkeling experience with the possibility of encountering spinner dolphins.

6.2 THE CAST OF CHARACTERS: MARINE LIFE IN MAUI'S CORAL REEFS

Now, let's meet the stars of the show—the diverse marine life that calls Maui's waters home. The underwater world is a spectacle of colors and shapes, from the tiniest reef fish to majestic sea turtles.

- **Hawaiian State Fish (Humuhumunukunukuapua'a):** The official state fish of Hawaii is the Humuhumunukunukuapua'a, often referred to as the reef triggerfish. Its distinctive name is derived from Hawaiian, meaning "fish with a snout like a pig." The Humuhumunukunukuapua'a is characterized by its striking colors and unique pattern, making it a favorite among locals and visitors. Its body showcases shades of blue, green, and yellow, contributing to its vibrant and eye-catching appearance. The reef triggerfish is commonly found in shallow coral reefs, lagoons, and coastal areas around the Hawaiian Islands, making it a symbolic and cherished representative of Hawaii's marine life. Ok one more time just for practice: Humuhumunukunukuapua'a.

- **Hawaiian Green Sea Turtle (Honu):** The gentle and iconic Hawaiian green sea turtle is a frequent sight while snorkeling in Maui. These ancient creatures gracefully navigate the reefs, often gliding alongside snorkelers. Remember to maintain a respectful distance and observe without interference.

- **Humpback Whales (Koholā):** While snorkeling, you might be fortunate enough to hear the mesmerizing songs of humpback whales. Wherever you may be on a snorkel trip, make a point to submerge, close your eyes, and just listen. You will discover yet another magical element of this enchantingly unique world.

- **Yellow Tang (Lau'ipala):** One of the most recognizable reef fish, the yellow tang, adds a burst of sunshine to Maui's underwater landscapes. These small, bright yellow fish with striking blue accents create a captivating contrast against the coral backdrop.

- **Parrotfish (Uhu):** With their vibrant colors and beak-like mouths, parrotfish are a common sight in Maui's coral reefs. These herbivores play a crucial role in maintaining the health of the reefs by grazing on algae, and their eclectic colors make them a delight for snorkelers.

- **Moorish Idol (Kihikihi):** Named after the Moors of Africa, the Moorish idol is a striking fish with its distinctive long, trailing dorsal fin. Spotting one of these elegant fish gliding through the water is a memorable experience.
- **Spinner Dolphins (Nai'a):** These playful dolphins are known for their acrobatic displays and often frequent the waters around Maui. While snorkeling, keep an eye out for pods of these dolphins, which are known for their somersaults and spins.
- **Hawaiian Monk Seal (Ilio-holo-i-ka-uaua):** The Hawaiian monk seal, one of the rarest seal species in the world, occasionally graces Maui's shores. While snorkeling, it's a rare and special treat to spot these critically endangered creatures resting on the sandy ocean floor.
- **Eels (puhi)** Maui's coral reefs are home to a fascinating variety of eels, each with unique characteristics. The most common is the **Moray Eel,** found in a range of colors and sizes, notorious for their fearsome appearance with wide-open mouths, which is actually how they breathe. Then there's the **Dragon Moray Eel,** a rare sight, celebrated for its striking colors and dragon-like appearance. With its white and yellow pattern, the Snowflake Eel adds a touch of whimsy to the underwater landscape. These eels usually hide in crevices during the day, emerging at night to hunt, playing a vital role in the reef ecosystem by controlling fish populations and cleaning up dead animals.

- **The Blacktip Reef Shark (manō niho ‘ilio)** is a fascinating and iconic species commonly found in tropical coral reef environments, including the waters around Hawaii and Maui. The Blacktip Reef Shark is named for the distinctive black tips on its dorsal fin and other fins. It has a streamlined body, a pointed snout, and a bronze to grayish coloration on its upper side, fading to white on the underside. These sharks typically grow to a length of around 5 to 6 feet, although some individuals may reach up to 8 feet.

If I may take an opportunity to digress about one of the more hilarious sounds you may have never imagined...

I spent a winter working as a Naturalist for the Pacific Whale Foundation. Aside from afternoon and evening Whale Watch trips where I was found to be rambling into the microphone about all things magnificent about whales, the first trip of the day was a three-hour snorkel tour. A three-hour tour. Usually, we hit a couple of stops, but pretty much always, the first was going to be Molokini. Molokini Crater is a busy tourist spot, but for good reason, as its unique geology of being a shallow water reef directly adjacent to deep water ocean attracts a lot of Manta rays and some other species you might not see in 'regular' shore reefs. I've been very lucky to swim with manta rays, monk seals, and whale sharks there! It is also a regular home to blacktip reef sharks.

At about 10 AM on any given day, 15-20 snorkel tour boats are likely lining the crater, with a couple hundred snorkelers in the water. Most of them aren't aware that blacktip reef sharks are harmless, and even when the one that swims beneath them is only four feet long, the sound that emanates from 200 snorkels simultaneously...Some snorkel yelps, some snorkel screams, some snorkel gasps, hoots and hollers... I can't appropriately put it to words, but this collective sound is gloriously hilarious!

Here's a fun fact: Did you know sharks have existed on planet Earth longer than trees, by 80 million years!? Not too shabby!

6.3 OCTOPI

While the Hawaiian Islands are home to a vast variety of marine life, including fascinating cephalopods, octopuses are not native to Hawaii's waters. Octopuses are more commonly found in colder waters, and Hawaii's warm tropical environment is not ideal for most octopus species. However, other cephalopods, such as squid and cuttlefish, inhabit the surrounding waters.

- **Hawaiian Bobtail Squid:** The Hawaiian bobtail squid is a small species native to the central Pacific, including the waters around Maui. It is recognizable by its translucent body and large, distinctive eyes. This nocturnal squid has a symbiotic relationship with bioluminescent bacteria, which it uses for camouflage by matching the ambient light.
- **Day Octopus:** While not specific to Maui, the day octopus can be found in the warm waters of the Hawaiian Islands, and snorkelers or divers may occasionally encounter them. These octopuses are excellent hunters, feeding on small crustaceans and

fish. They are known for their intelligence and ability to change color and texture for camouflage.

- **Hawaiian Octopus:** Often called the Night Octopus due to its nocturnal habits, this species resides in the reefs around Maui. Smaller and more elusive than the Day Octopus, it's a master of camouflage.
- **Bigfin Reef Squid:** This cephalopod species is found in tropical and subtropical waters and may be encountered in Hawaii, including the waters around Maui. Its elongated body and distinctive large fins make it an agile and swift swimmer.

Observing Cephalopods in Maui: If you're interested in observing cephalopods in Maui, particularly while snorkeling or diving, it's essential to be patient and attentive to your surroundings. Cephalopods are known for their ability to change color and texture, making them masters of camouflage. Look for them in areas with rocky substrates, coral reefs, and seagrass beds where they may find shelter and food.

Remember to practice responsible wildlife viewing. Keep a respectful distance, avoid touching or disturbing these animals, and never attempt to capture them. Observing cephalopods in their natural habitat is a thrilling experience contributing to the appreciation and conservation of marine life in Maui's waters.

6.4 CORAL AND PLANT LIFE BENEATH THE WAVES

Maui's underwater landscapes are not just populated by animals; they are adorned with a variety of plant life, contributing to the delicate balance of the marine ecosystem.

First, I have a question: Is coral a plant or animal?

Coral is actually an animal, not a plant. Corals belong to the phylum Cnidaria, which also includes jellyfish and sea anemones. A coral "colony" consists of numerous individual animals known as polyps. These polyps are tiny, soft-bodied organisms that live together in groups, creating the larger structures we recognize as coral reefs by secreting calcium carbonate, which forms their hard, protective skeletons.

Despite their animal classification, corals have a unique relationship with a type of algae called zooxanthellae, which live inside their tissues. This symbiotic relationship is what often confuses people about the nature of corals. The zooxanthellae photosynthesize, producing oxygen and other nutrients that the coral polyps need to live. In return, the coral provides the algae with a protected environment and the compounds necessary for photosynthesis. This mutually beneficial relationship allows corals to thrive in nutrient-poor tropical waters and is a key reason why coral reefs are so vibrant and diverse, supporting a vast array of other marine life.

- **Cauliflower Coral** stands out with its distinctive, lumpy texture and branching shape, resembling its namesake vegetable. Its color can range from pink to yellowish-green, adding a splash of color to the underwater landscape.

- **Lobe Coral** which forms large, dome-shaped structures that can span several feet in diameter. These massive corals are slow-growing, adding just a few millimeters each year, and their extensive colonies serve as important habitats for a myriad of marine life.
- **The Blue Rice Coral** is a rarer sight, prized for its unique blue hue. This species contributes to the reef's diversity and structural complexity, offering shelter and food to a wide variety of fish and invertebrates.
- **Finger Coral** creates delicate, finger-like projections that weave through the reef, providing intricate passageways and hideouts for small creatures.

These coral species, among others, form the backbone of Maui's reefs, supporting biodiversity and protecting the islands' shorelines. They are vital to marine life and the cultural and economic well-being of Maui's communities, underscoring the importance of coral reef conservation.

- **Seagrasses:** These underwater meadows serve as important feeding and breeding grounds for many marine species. Snorkelers might glimpse the swaying blades of seagrasses, which shelter juvenile fish and provide a food source for herbivores.
- **Hawaiian Sargass:** This unique type of brown algae is often found in Maui's coastal waters. Snorkelers might spot it floating on the surface or attached to

rocks, providing habitat and food for various marine creatures.

- **Halimeda Algae:** Known for its distinctive coin-like segments, halimeda algae contributes to the reef's calcium carbonate production. Its presence is not only visually interesting but also helps maintain the health of the coral ecosystem.

Coral Conservation and Responsible Snorkeling

While Maui's underwater world is a feast for the senses, it's essential to approach snorkeling with a mindset of conservation and responsibility. Coral reefs are delicate ecosystems facing numerous threats, including climate change, pollution, and overuse.

- **Coral-Safe Sunscreen:** When snorkeling in Maui, opt for coral-safe sunscreen to minimize the impact on the delicate coral reefs. Traditional sunscreens containing oxybenzone and octinoxate have been found to be harmful to coral, so choose alternatives labeled as reef-safe.
- **Responsible Wildlife Interaction:** Keep a respectful distance from marine life and avoid touching or chasing animals. This applies particularly to sea turtles, which are protected by law. Admire these creatures from a distance to ensure their well-being and preserve their natural behaviors.
- **Avoid Standing on Coral:** Although the reefs may look like a colorful underwater garden, resist the urge to stand on or touch the coral. Even a gentle touch can cause irreversible damage to these slow-

growing organisms. Instead, float above the reefs and enjoy the view without physical contact.

- **Support Conservation Efforts:** Consider supporting local marine conservation organizations and initiatives working to protect Maui's marine environment. Participate in beach cleanups, educational programs, or donate to organizations dedicated to preserving Hawaii's marine ecosystems.

Sources and Additional Reading

For those eager to delve deeper into the world of snorkeling in Maui, here are some recommended sources and further reading:

- **"Hawaii's Fishes: A Guide for Snorkelers and Divers" by John P. Hoover:** This comprehensive guidebook provides detailed information on the diverse fish species found in Hawaiian waters, including those around Maui.
- **Maui Ocean Center:** The Maui Ocean Center, located in Maalaea, is an excellent place to learn about Maui's marine life. Their exhibits and educational programs provide insights into the island's unique underwater ecosystems.
- **Reef Environmental Education Foundation (REEF):** REEF offers online courses and resources for those interested in marine conservation and responsible snorkeling. Their Fish Identification Program is a great way to enhance your knowledge of underwater species.

- **Hawaii Division of Aquatic Resources:** The official website of the Hawaii Division of Aquatic Resources provides up-to-date information on marine regulations, conservation efforts, and the latest news related to Hawaii's marine environment.

6.5 TURTLES!

Maui, Hawaii, isn't just a paradise for sun-seekers and surfers; it's also a haven for some of the most charming and chill residents of the ocean: sea turtles. These ancient mariners have been cruising the Earth's oceans for about 110 million years, and when you spot one gliding gracefully through the waters of Maui, it's like getting a glimpse into the prehistoric past. But don't let their old age fool you; these creatures are as fascinating as they come.

In the warm and inviting waters around Maui, you're most likely to encounter two types of sea turtles: the Hawaiian Green Sea Turtle, known locally as "Honu," and the Hawksbill Turtle, known as "Honu'ea." Let's dive a bit deeper into the world of these oceanic old-timers.

Hawaiian Green Sea Turtle (Honu) The Honu is the poster child of Hawaiian sea turtles, frequently seen both by snorkelers and divers along the coastlines. These gentle giants can grow to about 4 feet in length and tip the scales at up to 300 pounds when fully grown. But despite their size, they're known for their peaceful and graceful swimming.

One of the coolest facts about these turtles is how long they can hold their breath. While chilling or sleeping underwater, they can go without a breath for a couple of hours. However, during a rigorous activity, like avoiding a snorkeler eager for a selfie, they'll need to come up for air every few minutes.

Green Sea Turtles are known for their longevity, living up to 80 years or more. That's a lot of ocean to explore in a lifetime! They're also remarkable navigators, with females returning to the exact beach where they were hatched to lay their eggs.

Hawksbill Turtle (Honu'ea) The Honu'ea is much rarer and is recognized by its sharper, bird-like beak and beautifully patterned shell. These turtles are smaller than their green cousins, growing up to about 3 feet in length and weighing around 100 to 150 pounds. Hawksbills are considered critically endangered, so spotting one in Maui is a special treat.

These turtles have a bit of a gourmet palate, preferring to dine on sponges and other invertebrates that other sea creatures tend to avoid. This selective diet plays a crucial role in maintaining the health of coral reefs.

Hawksbill Turtles also have impressive breath-holding abilities and can stay underwater for up to three hours while resting. Like the Green Sea Turtles, they're long-lived, with lifespans that can stretch beyond 50 years.

Sea Turtle Fun Facts:

- Sea turtles are known to travel thousands of miles through the ocean, but they have a homing instinct that brings them back to their birthplace.
- Despite their hefty size, sea turtles are surprisingly fast swimmers, with some species reaching speeds up to 22 miles per hour!

- Turtles don't have teeth. Instead, they use their powerful jaws to crush or tear their food.

Conservation Success Stories

The efforts to protect Maui's dolphins and turtles have seen notable successes, thanks in part to the dedication of local conservation groups and the involvement of the community and visitors. The Hawaiian green sea turtle, once facing threats from hunting and habitat loss, has seen a significant increase in population numbers due to protected status and conservation initiatives. Similarly, education and protective measures have helped maintain healthy dolphin populations, ensuring that these intelligent creatures continue to thrive in Maui's waters.

The encounters we have with dolphins and turtles in Maui are more than just memorable moments; they're opportunities to connect with the marine world in a way that respects and preserves its wonders. Through understanding and responsible practices, we can ensure that future visitors will have the same chance to experience the magic of these encounters. And as we move forward, let us carry with us the lessons learned from these gentle creatures, reminding us of the beauty and fragility of the natural world.

LIFE ABOVE WATER

The air is crisp, filled with the promise of a new day. Suddenly, a melody breaks the silence—a song so pure and clear it could only belong to one of Maui's feathered residents. Welcome to a realm where each chirp, each whistle, and each flutter is a celebration of the island's dynamic ecosystem—the avian world of Maui.

7.1 BIRDSONG AT DAWN: BIRDS OF MAUI

Maui, a haven for bird enthusiasts, is home to a captivating array of bird species, each with its own unique traits and behaviors. Among these is the **Nēnē**, or **Hawaiian Goose**, Hawaii's state bird, uniquely adapted to life in the volcanic landscapes. Unlike other geese, the Nēnē has reduced webbing on its feet, suitable for walking on rugged terrain. Its soft calls echo across the islands.

The ʻIʻiwi, or **Scarlet Honeycreeper**, dazzles with its vivid red plumage and curved bill, perfectly shaped for sipping nectar from tubular flowers. This adaptation showcases the incredible evolutionary paths island life can take. The ʻIʻiwiʻs ability to hover like a hummingbird while feeding makes it a marvel of avian design.

Another notable resident is the **Hawaiian Hawk**, or ʻIo, considered sacred in Hawaiian culture. The ʻIo symbolizes royalty and power, a testament to its keen hunting skills and sharp vision. It's one of the few raptors endemic to Hawaii, demonstrating remarkable intelligence in its hunting strategies, often using the terrain to its advantage.

Lastly, the **Pacific Golden Plover, or Kōlea, is a master navigator. It makes** an astonishing annual migration of over 2,500 miles from Alaska to Hawaii without fail. These birds have an incredible internal compass, guiding them across vast oceans to the same Hawaiian Islands each year, a feat that continues to amaze scientists and bird lovers alike.

While rare, the luckiest of bird watchers on Maui might occasionally catch a glimpse of an **Albatross**. These birds are the definition of AWESOME.

The albatross is a marvel of the avian world, embodying the spirit of the open ocean. Among the largest of flying birds, some species like the **Wandering Albatross** have wingspans reaching up to 11 feet, the widest of any bird. These extensive wings enable them to glide effortlessly over the sea for hours, even days, without flapping, utilizing wind currents to conserve energy.

Albatrosses are renowned for their extraordinary migratory journeys, covering thousands of miles across oceans. They have a unique technique called dynamic soaring, which allows them to exploit wind gradients near the ocean's surface, essentially flying without limit. Some birds have been recorded traveling over 10,000 miles in a single journey.

Their social behavior is equally fascinating. Albatrosses engage in elaborate courtship dances, which include synchronized movements, calls, and beak clapping. These rituals are not only captivating but also form long-lasting pair bonds, with some species mating for life. The albatross's ability to navigate vast distances back to their breeding sites is another testament to their incredible navigation skills, making them one of the most remarkable navigators of the animal kingdom.

Birdwatching Hotspots

Timing and location are key to maximize your chances of spotting these rare birds. Early morning is prime bird-watching time when the island is just waking up. The forests are alive with song, and the birds are active, foraging for their morning meal.

- **Hosmer Grove in Haleakalā National Park**: A place where native forest birds thrive, offering an accessible trail that wanders through a unique mix of native and introduced trees.
- **Kealia Pond National Wildlife Refuge**: This coastal wetland area becomes a birder's paradise, especially during the winter months when migratory birds join the local population.

- **Waikamoi Preserve**: Managed by The Nature Conservancy, this area offers guided birdwatching tours that can give you a better shot at seeing some of the island's most elusive birds.

Interactive Element: Maui Birdwatching Checklist

Turn your birdwatching into a fun, interactive game with a printable checklist of Maui's endemic and common bird species. Tally your sightings and track when and where you spotted each bird. It's a great way to document your encounters and learn more about the island's avian residents.

Birdwatching is an invitation to become a steward of these magnificent creatures and their habitats. So, as you step into the world of birdwatching on Maui, do so with a sense of wonder and a commitment to tread lightly on the earth. The birds you seek are not just species to be checked off a list; they are fellow travelers on this planet, each with its own story, contributing to the miracle of life that makes Maui truly magical.

7.2 FLORA OF THE GODS: NATIVE PLANTS AND THEIR USES

Maui thrives with an array of plant life that beautifies its landscapes and plays a pivotal role in the island's cultural and ecological fabric. The native plant species of Maui are a bridge to the island's past, each with stories to tell and wisdom to impart, rooted deeply in the Hawaiian way of life.

Native Plant Species

The diversity of Maui's plant life is a mirror to the island's varied climates and topography. From the coastal **naupaka**, with its half-flower appearance, to the majestic **koa** trees in the upland forests, these plants have adapted to their environments in fascinating ways. The **ōhiʻa lehua**, with its vibrant red blossoms, is often one of the first plants to colonize new lava flows, symbolizing new life and growth. These native species are more than just flora; they are keystones of their ecosystems, providing habitat and food for a variety of wildlife.

Traditional Uses

For generations, the native people of Maui have turned to the island's plants for their daily needs, knowledge that is both profound and practical. The **kalo (taro)** plant, for instance, is at the heart of Hawaiian cuisine and culture, its roots transformed into poi in a process passed down through generations. The versatile **lauhala**, or **pandanus** leaf, is crafted into mats, baskets, and hats, an example of the ingenuity of traditional Hawaiian crafts. Medicinal uses also abound; the **noni** fruit is known for its healing properties, while the **mamaki** plant makes a soothing tea believed to cleanse the body and spirit.

Botanical Gardens and Reserves

For those eager to immerse themselves in the world of Maui's plants, the island offers sanctuaries where native flora is protected and celebrated. The **Kahanu Garden**, nestled in the coastal district of Hāna, is home to one of the largest collections of breadfruit in the world, along with other native and Polynesian-introduced plants. Visitors can walk among plants that have sustained Hawaiian communities for centuries. The **Maui Nui Botanical Gardens**, located in the heart of Kahului, is dedicated to the conservation of Maui's native and culturally significant plants. It's a place of learning and discovery, where each plant comes with a story, offering insights into Hawaii's botanical heritage and the efforts to preserve it.

For those drawn to upland forests, the **Hosmer Grove** in Haleakalā National Park showcases a range of native and introduced trees, a living laboratory of ecology and conservation. Meanwhile, the **Ke'anae Arboretum** offers a peaceful retreat along the Road to Hāna, where taro fields and wild ginger line the paths and rainbow eucalyptus paints the landscape with its multicolored bark.

These botanical havens are more than just places to admire the beauty of Maui's plants; they are gateways to understanding the deep connections between the island's flora, its people, and their shared history. They remind us that plants are not merely passive inhabitants of the landscape but active participants in Maui's story, shaping its culture, economy, and ecosystems.

In the Shadow of Giants: The Silversword and Other Alpine Flora

High above the lush landscapes and beachfronts that most associate with Maui, there exists an entirely different world. In the alpine zones, where the air is thinner and the temperatures are cooler, a unique community of plants has made a home. Among them, the Silversword stands out not just for its striking appearance but also for its incredible adaptation to the harsh conditions of its environment.

The Silversword, or `**Ahinahina** as known in Hawaiian, is a marvel of evolution. Its rosette of silvery leaves, designed to minimize water loss and reflect harsh sunlight, reflects nature's ingenuity. Blooming only once in its lifetime, which can span up to fifty years, the Silversword's flowering is a spectacle, drawing a crown of purple flowers that can be seen dotting the slopes of Haleakalā. This plant is not merely surviving; it's thriving, but not without facing significant challenges.

The alpine ecosystem of Maui is as delicate as it is beautiful. Plants have carved out niches among the volcanic rocks, each species contributing to a fragile web of life that sustains this high-altitude community. Alongside the Silversword, other specialized plants, such as the `**Ohelo** berry, with its edible red fruits, and the **Mauna Kea Silversword**, a cousin to Maui's Silversword, paint a picture of a unique, if vulnerable, ecosystem.

Exploring the alpine regions of Maui offers a glimpse into a world far removed from the island's beaches and forests. Here, in the shadow of giants like Haleakalā, the Silversword and its companions have a life in the face of adversity. Their existence is a reminder of the resilience of nature and the responsibility we share to protect these unique habitats. As you move through these landscapes, let the sight of a Silversword in bloom be a moment of awe and reflection, a symbol of Maui's rich biodiversity and the collective efforts to preserve it for future generations.

7.3 THE WILD BOAR AND THE GECKO: MAUI'S MAMMALS AND REPTILES

In the lush landscapes of Maui, the island's mammals and reptiles play their roles in the ecological theater with quiet determination. Among these creatures, the wild boar and the gecko might capture our imagination most vividly, each for different reasons. While one treads the undergrowth, leaving traces of its passage, the other clings to the walls of our homes, a silent observer of our daily lives.

The **Wild Boar**, or **Pua'a**, was introduced by early Polynesian settlers. These animals have played a significant role in Hawaiian culture, featuring in many traditional stories and practices. Wild boars are known for their intelligence and adaptability, thriving in Maui's forests, and even influencing the local ecosystem through their foraging habits, which can lead to soil disturbance and the spread of non-native plant species.

On the reptilian front, the **Gold Dust Day Gecko** is a colorful and charismatic character in Maui's animal community. Originally from Madagascar and introduced to Hawaii, these geckos are easily recognized by their vibrant green skin and red spots. They exhibit fascinating behaviors, such as vocalizations for communication and territorial defense. Geckos also play an essential role in controlling insect populations, showcasing their importance in maintaining ecological balance.

The **Hawaiian Hoary Bat**, or ʻŌpeʻapeʻa, is Hawaii's only native mammal and a true nocturnal navigator. This elusive bat is crucial for the island's ecosystem, acting as a natural pest controller. Using echolocation, it skillfully maneuvers through the night sky to catch insects. Interestingly, the ʻŌpeʻapeʻa is also recognized as a symbol of longevity and endurance in Hawaiian culture, admired for its ability to thrive in various habitats across the islands.

While Hawaii lacks native amphibians, the **Coqui Frog**, an introduced species, has become a common presence. Originally from Puerto Rico, the Coqui's loud, distinctive call is now part of the island's soundscape. Despite being considered invasive, the Coqui frog's rapid adaptation to Maui's environment is a testament to its resilience and survival skills.

Each of these species, from the native ʻŌpeʻapeʻa to the introduced Gold Dust Day Gecko, plays a unique role in Maui's ecosystem. Their behaviors and adaptations offer a glimpse into the complexity of natural life on the island, highlighting the interconnectedness of all living beings and the importance of conservation efforts to preserve this diversity for future generations.

Human-Wildlife Interactions

The relationship between humans and wildlife in Maui is delicate. As the island's human footprint expands, finding ways to coexist with these native and introduced species becomes increasingly important. For example, initiatives to control the wild boar population through hunting and fencing aim to protect native flora without eradicating a culturally significant species. Similarly, guidelines for inter-acting with sea turtles and monk seals help ensure that our presence doesn't disturb these vulnerable creatures.

Protecting Maui's Wildlife

Conservation efforts in Maui are a demonstration of the island's commitment to its non-human residents. From habitat restoration projects that offer a lifeline to the Hawaiian hoary bat to marine protected areas that safeguard green sea turtles and their nesting sites, these initiatives reflect a broader understanding of our role in the natural world. It's here, in the actions we take to preserve and protect, that we find the true measure of our relationship with the island's wildlife.

TRAILS LESS TRAVELED

8.1 THE BAMBOO FOREST'S WHISPER

Maui's bamboo forests are ethereal, offering a serene and almost mystical experience. Among the best is the bamboo forest found along the **Pipiwai Trail**, located in the Kipahulu District of Haleakalā National Park. As you venture into this lush, verdant landscape, the towering bamboo stalks create a natural cathedral, their leaves whispering in the wind like soft rain. The trail itself is a moderately challenging hike that rewards adventurers with not just the bamboo forest, but also views of cascading waterfalls, including the majestic 400-foot **Waimoku Falls** at the trail's end. The sunlight filters through the dense canopy, casting a gentle, green glow that illuminates the path. The sound of the bamboo stalks clattering together in the breeze is enchanting, providing an atmosphere that enhances the sense of isolation and tranquility. This bamboo forest is not just a hike; it's an immersive experience that showcases Maui's natural beauty and the magic of its landscapes.

Flora and Fauna

As you weave your way through the bamboo, the forest reveals its diverse inhabitants. Look closely, and you may spot the flitting form of the 'I'iwi, a bird adorned with feathers as red as the setting sun, navigating the bamboo labyrinth with ease. Their distinct calls complementing the rustle of bamboo, enrich the forest's auditory glory. The ground beneath your feet, a lush of ferns and soft mosses, is alive with insects that buzz and burrow, each species intricately linked to the bamboo's lifecycle. In this hidden world, the bamboo transcends its role as a mere plant; it becomes the cornerstone of a complex ecosystem, nurturing a web of life that is as intricate as it is beautiful.

8.2 CRATERS AND CRESTS: HALEAKALA'S HIKING TRAILS

Stepping onto Haleakala's trails is like walking on the moon, with vast craters and ancient lava flows painting a picture of the island's fiery past. This silent giant, standing guard over Maui, offers adventurers a peek into the heart of the earth, where volcanic forces once raged with incredible power.

Volcanic Majesty

Haleakala Crater, a colossal depression left by volcanic activity, isn't just a geological wonder—it's a sacred place that captivates the imagination. Hiking here, you traverse landscapes that range from stark, barren deserts to vibrant, life-bursting zones where nature has claimed its territory back from the ash. It's in these contrasts that Haleakala reveals its true beauty, a reflection of the earth's ability to create and destroy, to wipe the slate clean and start anew. The terrain here tells stories of eruptions that shaped the island, offering a unique opportunity to connect with Maui's primal forces.

Sunrise Hikes

Witnessing the sunrise from the summit of Haleakala is an ethereal experience transcending mere words. As dawn breaks, the vast sky transitions from a deep indigo to a mesmerizing palette of pinks and golds, bathing the crater's rugged landscape in a soft, otherworldly light. This spectacle offers a panoramic vista that extends beyond the crater, reaching the infinite horizon of the Pacific Ocean.

Trail Selection

Haleakala's trails cater to a wide range of interests and abilities, from short walks that offer a taste of the crater's majesty to multi-day treks that delve deep into its heart. Selecting the right trail can turn a hike into an unforgettable adventure:

- **For the Time-Pressed**: The Pa Ka'oao Trail offers a short, accessible hike with rewarding views of the crater. It's perfect for those wanting a glimpse of Haleakala's majesty without the commitment of a full-day hike.
- **Moderate Adventurers**: Sliding Sands Trail provides a more in-depth exploration of the crater, descending into its depths and revealing the vibrant colors and textures of this volcanic landscape. It's a

moderate hike that requires a bit of stamina but pays off in spectacular views.

- **Seasoned Hikers**: Those seeking a challenge might tackle the Halemau'u Trail, a strenuous route that rewards hikers with unparalleled vistas and encounters with endemic flora and fauna. It's a journey that demands respect for the mountain's rugged terrain but offers rich rewards in return.

Choosing your path wisely, considering not just the physical challenge but also the time and the landscapes you wish to experience, turns a hike into a journey of discovery.

8.3 WATERFALLS AND WONDERS: EAST MAUI'S HIDDEN GEMS

East Maui, known for its lush landscapes and the winding Road to Hana, is home to some of the most stunning waterfalls in Hawaii. Among these, the **Seven Sacred Pools at 'Ohe'o Gulch** stand out, offering a series of cascading waterfalls and tranquil pools that invite visitors for a refreshing dip. Nestled within the Haleakalā National Park, this natural wonder is a display of Maui's volcanic history and the erosive power of water over millennia.

Another gem is the towering worth mentioning at least a couple of times in this book is **Waimoku Falls**, which plunges 400 feet down a sheer lava rock face, creating a dramatic backdrop against the dense bamboo forest it cuts through. The journey to Waimoku is an adventure itself, accessible via the **Pipiwai Trail,** a path that weaves through lush rainforest, past banyan trees, and alongside smaller cascades, making it a rewarding trek for those seeking the awe of nature's force.

Not to be overlooked, **Twin Falls** serves as the gateway to East Maui's waterfall country. Easily accessible and family-friendly, these falls offer the perfect introduction to the island's rich aquatic landscapes. With its inviting pools and serene surroundings, Twin Falls encapsulates the enchanting beauty of East Maui, making it a must-visit for anyone exploring the island's natural treasures.

Cultural Significance

Waterfalls in Maui are more than mere natural attractions; they are steeped in the rich culture of the island. Locals regard these places with reverence, often associated with the 'aina (land) that sustains them. The story of the demigod Maui, who, in his quest to slow the sun, is said to have formed the island's many valleys and waterfalls with his mighty blows, imbues these locations with a mythic quality. Understanding these stories deepens the appreciation for each visit, turning a simple hike into a journey through the living history and culture of Maui.

7.4 FOOT TRAILS OF WEST MAUI

West Maui, with its rugged terrain and panoramic views, boasts some of the island's most breathtaking hiking trails. The pinnacle of these treks is the **Waihe'e Ridge Trail**, which offers hikers a challenging ascent through lush forests, leading to unparalleled views of the Waihe'e Valley and the sparkling Pacific Ocean. This 5-mile round-trip hike rewards the adventurous with vistas of steep mountain ridges and distant waterfalls, culminating in a scenic overlook at the summit.

Another highlight is the **Lahaina Pali Trail**, a historic path that winds its way over the West Maui Mountains. This strenuous 5-mile trek is not for the faint of heart, but those who undertake it are rewarded with sweeping views of Maalaea Bay, the central valley, and the neighboring islands of Lanai and Molokai. The trail's rocky terrain and steep inclines make it a formidable challenge, but the panoramic views at the summit are a worthy payoff.

For those seeking a less intense but equally rewarding experience, the **Kapalua Coastal Trail** is a scenic alternative. This gentle 3.5-mile walk skirts the coastline, offering stunning ocean views, access to secluded beaches, and glimpses of marine life. The trail passes through luxury resorts and native vegetation, showcasing the diverse beauty of West Maui's landscapes.

CANOEING, SURFING AND SCUBA DIVING

I magine yourself on the glowing shores of Maui, with your toes sinking into the warm, golden sand. The air is laced with the tang of sea salt, and the vast, boundless Pacific Ocean is before you. It is here, amidst the rhythmic ebb and flow of the azure waves, that you encounter a tale woven into the very fabric of time—surfing. This pursuit transcends mere sport; it embodies a profound legacy and a pulsating rhythm that beats at the core of Hawaiian culture, connecting past and present in each glide across the water's surface.

9.1 STELLAR SURF SPOTS

Maui boasts some of the world's most renowned surfing spots, each offering a unique blend of waves, scenery, and local culture that appeals to surfers of all skill levels. From the gentle rollers perfect for beginners to the towering waves challenging even the most seasoned professionals, Maui's coastlines serve as a surfers' paradise. Here's a comprehensive guide to the best surfing spots on this enchanting island.

- **Honolua Bay:** Nestled on the northwest shore, Honolua Bay is a world-class surfing destination known for its right-hand point break. During the winter months, the bay offers large, perfectly shaped waves that attract professional surfers and spectators from around the globe. The clear, turquoise water and abundant marine life also make it a popular spot for snorkeling during calmer conditions. However, due to its popularity and the quality of waves, Honolua Bay is recommended for experienced surfers.
- **Hookipa Beach:** Situated on Maui's north shore, Hookipa Beach is famously known as the "windsurfing capital of the world," but its waves are equally appealing to surfers. The beach features several breaks that can accommodate surfers of various skill levels, with the winter months offering the most consistent conditions. Besides the thrilling waves, Hookipa Beach is also a great place to observe Hawaiian green sea turtles basking on the sand.
- **Pe'ahi (Jaws):** Pe'ahi, or Jaws, is synonymous with big wave surfing. Located on the north shore, Jaws is famous for its monstrous waves that can reach heights of up to 60 feet (18 meters) during the winter. This spot is strictly for professional and highly experienced surfers equipped with tow-in gear, as the waves here are powerful and the water currents extremely strong. The spectacle of surfers conquering these colossal waves makes Jaws a

popular spot for onlookers. Some of the biggest waves ever surfed in the world have been at Pe'ahi.

- **Lahaina Breakwall:** A favorite among beginner and intermediate surfers, Lahaina Breakwall offers a more sheltered and manageable surfing experience. Located in front of the historic Lahaina Harbor, this spot features long, slow-breaking waves ideal for longboarding and those looking to improve their surfing skills.
- **Ma'alaea Bay:** Known for the 'Freight Trains,' one of the world's fastest right-hand breaks, Ma'alaea Bay is a magnet for experienced surfers seeking a thrilling ride. The waves here are quick and powerful and barrel over a shallow coral reef, making it suitable only for those with expert skills. The best conditions are during the summer when south swells hit the bay.

Each spot encapsulates the diverse surfing experiences Maui has to offer, from serene, beginner-friendly waves to the adrenaline-pumping heights of professional-grade swells. Whether you're paddling out for the first time or looking to test your limits against some of the planet's most formidable waves, Maui's shores welcome all with open arms and promise an unforgettable surfing adventure.

Surfing Etiquette

Out here, respect is everything. The waves belong to no one and everyone. It's about taking turns and knowing when to go and give way. It's the nod to a fellow surfer as you paddle out, the shared stoke after a perfect ride. This unspoken code keeps the peace on the water and ensures everyone gets their moment with the ocean.

- **Right of Way**: The surfer closest to the peak of the wave has dibs. Simple as that.
- **Don't Drop In**: Cutting in front of someone already on a wave? That's a no-go.
- **Paddle Wide**: Keep clear of the path of surfers riding waves when paddling back out.

These rules aren't just about order; they're about honoring the spirit of surfing, ensuring it remains a joy for all.

Surf Schools

For those keen to dive into Maui's surfing culture, many schools offer more than just technique; they offer a passage into the soul of surfing. Choosing the right school means finding instructors who not only teach you how to stand on a board but also share the stories, history, and respect for the ocean that define surfing in Maui.

- **Goofy Foot Surf School** is known for its personalized approach, which ensures that every student catches not just waves but the essence of surfing.
- **Maui Surf Clinics**: Offers a deep dive into surfing's cultural roots, connecting students with the sport's rich Hawaiian heritage.

Picking up a board and hitting the waves with these schools isn't just a lesson; it's an initiation into an ancient lineage of ocean lovers.

9.2 KITE SURFING: EMBRACING THE WIND

Kite surfing brings an unmatched rush, transforming Maui's gusts into a fuel that propels you across the open sea. This sport, a blend of wakeboarding, surfing, paragliding, and gymnastics, taps into the power of the wind, offering a thrilling way to sail with the ocean's waves.

Maui's shores are a paradise for those eager to harness the wind's energy. The island's consistent trade winds and diverse coastal landscapes make it ideal for kitesurfing. From the gentle breezes of the North Shore to the stronger gusts found at spots like Kanaha Beach Park, Maui provides a variety of conditions suitable for every experience level.

- **Kanaha Beach Park**: Renowned for its reliable winds and large, open areas, it's perfect for beginners and intermediates to spread their wings.
- **Kihei**: The south side's answer to kitesurfing offers a different wind direction and usually lighter breezes, ideal for those looking to refine their technique in calmer conditions.

Wind conditions and safety should be paramount when choosing a location. Spots with steady onshore or side-shore winds are preferable, reducing the risk of being blown out to sea. Always check local forecasts and consult with experienced kitesurfers or instructors to find the day's best location.

The ocean is a shared space, home to countless marine species that rely on its resources. Kitesurfing, while exhilarating, should be done with mindfulness towards these underwater inhabitants. Avoid kitesurfing near coral reefs and marine protected areas, where the sport's impact can harm sensitive ecosystems. By staying informed about and adhering to local guidelines, you contribute to preserving Maui's rich marine life.

For those new to the sport, getting started in kitesurfing might seem daunting. However, Maui's welcoming community and abundant resources make it an accessible adventure for anyone willing to learn. Here are a few tips for beginners:

- **Choosing the Right Equipment**: Your kite's size will depend on your weight and the wind conditions. Beginners should opt for a larger board for stability. Safety gear, including a helmet and a life vest, is non-negotiable.
- **Finding the Right Instructor**: Look for certified instructors who prioritize safety and deeply understand Maui's winds and waters. Schools like Action Sports Maui and Hawaiian Kiteboarding Association offer lessons that emphasize technique, ocean awareness, and respect for the environment.
- **First Steps**: Your first lessons will cover the basics, from setting up your kite to understanding wind dynamics and safety procedures. Mastery comes with patience and practice, so give yourself time to learn and enjoy the process.

Kitesurfing in Maui isn't just about the thrill of riding the waves; it's a way to connect with the island's natural beauty and ocean sports traditions. Where the sky meets the sea, you find not just adrenaline but a profound sense of freedom and connection to the world around you.

9.3 CANOEING

Canoeing in Maui is not just a recreational activity; it's an integral part of Hawaiian culture and history, deeply rooted in the traditions of the Polynesian navigators who first discovered the Hawaiian Islands. These early settlers voyaged across vast expanses of the Pacific Ocean in double-hulled canoes, using the stars, ocean currents, and bird flight patterns for navigation. This legacy is preserved in Maui through the practice of outrigger canoe paddling, a sport that symbolizes the strength, unity, and resilience of the Hawaiian people.

Today, canoeing in Maui offers both locals and visitors an opportunity to connect with the island's rich heritage and stunning natural beauty. Paddling along Maui's clear, turquoise waters provides a unique perspective of the island's diverse marine life, volcanic landscapes, and serene beaches. Organizations and clubs often host cultural events and canoe races, fostering community spirit and honoring the traditions of their ancestors. Participating in or observing these events offers a deep appreciation for the skill, teamwork, and spiritual connection to the ocean that canoeing embodies in Hawaiian culture.

9.4 DEPTHS UNSEEN: SPECTACULAR SCUBA DIVING SPOTS

Underwater Exploration

Maui is a scuba diver's paradise, offering an astonishing array of underwater experiences. From vibrant coral reefs to mysterious wrecks and unique volcanic formations, Maui's underwater world is teeming with life and color. Among the numerous scuba diving spots near Maui, a few stand out for their exceptional beauty and the diversity of marine life they host.

Molokini Crater is undoubtedly one of the most famous scuba diving spots near Maui. This partially submerged volcanic crater forms a natural aquarium, providing shelter to a vast array of marine life. Visibility here can exceed 100 feet, offering crystal-clear views of over 250 species of fish and a variety of coral species. Divers might spot the rare Hawaiian monk seal and manta rays, and during the winter months, they may even hear the song of migrating humpback whales.

Lanai Cathedrals, a short boat ride from Maui, offers one of the most spectacular dive experiences. The First and Second Cathedrals are large, underwater lava tubes that resemble gothic cathedrals, complete with arches and windows through which sunlight filters, creating a surreal underwater light show. Divers can expect to see abundant marine life, including spinner dolphins, eagle rays, and the occasional turtle passing by.

Turtle Town is another must-visit diving location near Maui, famous for its large population of Hawaiian green sea turtles. The area, encompassing Maluaka Beach, offers divers and snorkelers the chance to swim alongside these majestic creatures in their natural habitat. The underwater landscape is marked by a series of lava formations and coral gardens, home to a colorful variety of fish, eels, and occasionally, the shy octopus.

Five Caves near Makena is renowned for its underwater caverns and tunnels, offering an adventurous dive for those looking to explore Maui's undersea topography. The area is known for its diverse marine life, including vibrant butterfly fish, curious moray eels, and rare Hawaiian lionfish. The caves also provide safe environments for encountering larger marine animals, such as white-tip reef sharks and barracudas.

Honolua Bay, part of the Mokuleia Marine Life Conservation District, is a favorite among divers for its protected status and the abundance of marine life it supports. The bay offers excellent diving conditions with calm, clear waters and is home to a healthy coral reef ecosystem. Divers might find themselves swimming with schools of tropical fish, exploring the nooks and crannies for nudibranchs, or observing the graceful movements of sea turtles.

Marine Conservation

The beauty of Maui's underwater world is matched only by its fragility. Coral reefs, the ocean's rainforests, face threats from climate change, pollution, and human activities. Divers play a crucial role in the conservation of these ecosystems.

Participating in reef cleanups or citizen science projects helps monitor reef health and contributes to global efforts to protect these vital habitats. Organizations like the Maui Ocean Center Marine Institute work tirelessly to rehabilitate injured marine life and restore coral reefs, offering divers a chance to support conservation through volunteer opportunities. Every dive with a purpose adds to the collective effort to safeguard Maui's marine environments for future generations.

9.5 NIGHT SNORKELING: A DIFFERENT WORLD

Nocturnal Marvels

Beneath the veil of night, Maui's ocean transforms into a bustling community of marine life. Creatures that spend daylight hours hidden from view become emboldened under the cover of darkness, offering snorkelers a unique window into their nocturnal activities. The flashlight's glow reveals the dazzling spectacle of squid and eels as they weave through the water, their bodies casting iridescent glimmers in the beam. Meanwhile, the watchful gaze of an octopus emerges from its sanctuary, adding a touch of mystery to the underwater exploration. Night snorkeling transcends mere observation; it fosters a profound connection with the often unseen, vibrant ecosystem that flourishes beneath the ocean's surface, inviting snorkelers into a world brimming with wonder and discovery.

A BEACH LOVER'S PARADISE

10.1 – WHICH BEACH IS BEST?

It won't matter which of Maui's dozens of beautiful beaches you choose to spend your day on; you will surely have a great experience. Here are just some of the best:

- **Ka'anapali Beach**: Let's start with a classic – Ka'anapali Beach. Located on Maui's west coast, this three-mile stretch of golden sand is a postcard-perfect paradise. With its calm, clear waters and picture-perfect palm trees, it's no wonder Ka'anapali is a favorite among locals and tourists alike. Whether you're lounging on the sand, launching off Blackrock, snorkeling among the colorful coral reefs, or simply taking in the breathtaking views of Lanai and Molokai, Ka'anapali never fails to impress.
- **Wailea Beach**: Moving down the coast, we come to Wailea Beach – a true gem of South Maui.

Nestled between luxury resorts and swaying coconut palms, Wailea Beach is renowned for its powdery white sand and pristine turquoise waters. It's the perfect spot for swimming, paddleboarding, or simply soaking up the sun in style. And if you're lucky, you might even spot a humpback whale breaching in the distance during whale season.

- **Napili Bay**: Tucked away on Maui's northwest shore, Napili Bay is paradise waiting to be discovered. This crescent-shaped beach boasts calm, shallow waters ideal for swimming and snorkeling, making it a favorite among families and water sports enthusiasts. Pack a picnic, spread out your beach towel, and spend the day exploring the amazing underwater world just offshore.

- **Kapalua Bay**: Just around the corner from Napili Bay lies another Maui treasure – Kapalua Bay. With its sheltered cove and crystal-clear waters, Kapalua Bay is a snorkeler's paradise. The calm conditions and abundant marine life make it the perfect spot for beginners and experienced snorkelers alike. After a day of underwater exploration, be sure to stick around for one of Maui's famous sunsets – you won't regret it.

- **Ho'okipa Beach**: For those seeking a bit more adventure, Ho'okipa Beach on Maui's north shore is the place to be. Known as the windsurfing capital of the world, Ho'okipa's consistent trade winds and powerful waves attract adrenaline junkies from far and wide. Even if you're not hitting the waves yourself, watching the skilled surfers and windsurfers in action is an experience you won't soon forget.

- **Hamoa Beach**: As we make our way along the famous Road to Hana, we come to one of Maui's hidden gems – Hamoa Beach. Tucked away beneath lush cliffs and swaying coconut palms, Hamoa Beach is a postcard-perfect paradise. The crescent-shaped bay boasts soft, golden sand and clear blue waters, making it the perfect spot for swimming, sunbathing, or simply taking in the breathtaking scenery.
- **Big Beach (Makena Beach)**: Aptly named for its expansive stretch of golden sand, Big Beach – also known as Makena Beach – is a must-visit for beach lovers on Maui's south shore. Backed by towering cliffs and fringed by swaying palms, Big Beach is as picturesque as they come. Whether you're swimming in the turquoise waters, bodyboarding in the shore break, or simply lounging on the sand, Big Beach is the epitome of Maui's natural beauty.
- **Little Beach (Pu'u Olai Beach)**: Just a short walk from Big Beach lies another Maui treasure – Little Beach. Despite its name, Little Beach is big on charm, with its powdery white sand and turquoise waters. The beach is famous for its Sunday evening drum circles and clothing-optional policy, making it a favorite among free spirits and bohemian souls. Come for the sunset, stay for the music, and dance the night away beneath the stars.
- **Red Sand Beach (Kaihalulu Beach)**: For something truly unique, head to the secluded Red Sand Beach – also known as Kaihalulu Beach – in Hana. Accessible via a short but steep trail, Red Sand Beach is nestled

within a dramatic cove surrounded by towering cliffs and lush vegetation. The beach gets its name from its striking red sand, created by the iron-rich lava rock that lines the shore. It's a bit off the beaten path, but the journey is well worth the reward.

- **Honolua Bay**: Last but certainly not least, we come to Honolua Bay – a marine reserve and surf mecca on Maui's northwest coast. The bay's clear waters and coral reefs make it a haven for snorkelers and scuba divers, while its powerful winter swells draw experienced surfers from around the world. Whether you're paddling out to catch a wave or simply soaking up the sun on the rocky shore, Honolua Bay is a must-visit for anyone seeking adventure and natural beauty on Maui.

10.2 - LIFEGUARD TRAINING

Maybe it's time for another digression, as writing about Kapalua bay has triggered another 'fond' memory...

As previously mentioned, one of the times I moved to Maui was to work as a Naturalist for the Pacific Whale Foundation. To my surprise, this job would entail far more than just educating the public on whale trivia. I would also be leading snorkel reef tours which would mean being able to identify just about every critter that swims among Maui's reefs. As part of the 'boat crew', I would have to assist in securing the boat to underwater moorings, which would require a significant upgrade to my lung capacity and swimming legs. Oh yeah, I would also have to get certified as a lifeguard as an impressive number of people who don't really know how to swim sign up for snorkeling tours for some reason... Each of these responsibilities would necessitate considerable training.

So, shortly after my arrival on the island, I headed to Kapalua Bay on a bright sunny day to practice.

I was a bit disappointed to see conditions were a bit choppy and murky, thus diminishing my opportunity for fish ID practice. However, this was no problem as lung capacity training and strengthening swimming legs were a top priority.

To practice deeper free-diving, I swam pretty far out into the bay. About 30 minutes into my diving practice, during which I spent most of my time hanging out on the ocean floor, the swell doubled.

'The sea was angry that day my friends.'

I decided it was time to bug out, so I swam toward shore. I swam and swam. Sadly, every time I looked up to check my progress, it seemed I wasn't making any.

Having spent a good deal of time on beaches in my previous winter living on Maui, I had heard the advice a hundred times: if you get caught in a riptide, don't panic, and swim perpendicular to the shore and head in later.

I didn't panic. I swam to the right, but I still had no luck. Swimming to the left would eventually lead to my being smeared upon lava rock by the now triple-sized waves.

I still wasn't panicking (despite the ever-increasing swell), but I was starting to get tired, and there was a growing group of people on shore watching my lack of progress, and they

WERE starting to panic. After about ten more futile and exhausting minutes, I got hit by a LARGE wave unexpectedly, which caused me to inhale more than the daily doctor-recommended dose of seawater. Now adding choking to the mix, I finally was starting to panic. I looked to my still-growing legion of adoring fans on shore and gave the international lifeguard signal for 'help' and waived my arms over my head.

My fans on shore seemed to be frantically gesturing for me to swim straight out to sea to get past the now deadly breaking waves, so I did that.

And guess whose maybe-slightly-oversized-yet-still-delightfully-shapely-nitwit-ass got rescued by the Coast Guard?!

After my complimentary jet ski ride back to the beach... I sheepishly shuffled through the sand, past an array of wide-eyed tourists who had given me up for dead just two minutes prior, to a secluded back corner of the beach. I pondered my pride and started planning my now imminent move to Kansas.

About fifteen minutes later the ocean grew suddenly calm. Immediately the beach folk started heading back into the water. One of the folk was a guy holding his probably six-month-old child. As the pair got to the low point of the waterline, they turned to shore to pose for the camera. Then I noticed the 'Kahuna from Down Unda' about 5 seconds away.

I yelled to them and gave the internal lifeguard signal for: 'get the f**k out of there!' He heard me, turned to see impending doom, and froze in his tracks.

By the time the wave hit them it was a good 12-footer.

Luckily, another guy was also watching the situation unfold, and we were both at full tilt in their direction when the wave hit. The other guy grabbed the baby, who appeared to be grinning and delighted by the splashy water ride, and I pulled out the dad, who was so petrified he couldn't initially stand up on dry land.

I then proceeded to a nice patch of grass BEHIND the beach to try to relax as it was becoming a notably unrelaxing day.

Then I watched my savior, the jet ski guy, pluck out another tourist.

Then my savior the jet ski guy yelled to everyone that the beach was now closed.

Then I went home and had a double gin and tonic.

Is there a moral to this story? Cliche advice at least?

Don't turn your back on the ocean, she can be a bit fierce at times.

LIVING ALOHA THROUGH CUISINE AND CULTURE

Stepping into a bustling Maui market early in the morning, the air is cool, tinged with the scent of fresh produce and the earthy aroma of just-picked herbs and spices. Around you, locals greet each other with warm smiles and "howzits," sharing recipes and news over piles of vibrant fruits and vegetables. This isn't just shopping; it's a daily gathering that confirms the island's community spirit and deep-rooted connection to the land. Welcome to the farm-to-table movement in Maui, where every dish tells a story of tradition, sustainability, and the Aloha spirit.

11.1 FARM TO TABLE: THE MOVEMENT SHAPING MAUI'S CUISINE

Sustainable Agriculture

Maui's farmers are the unsung heroes of the island's culinary scene. They work tirelessly, often against the challenges of limited water and invasive species, to bring to the table produce that's as rich in flavor as it is in nutrients. Sustainable farming practices here go beyond just organic certification. They're about water conservation, soil health, and biodiversity – ensuring that the land can continue to nourish generations to come. It's a commitment to the 'aina (land) that feeds not just the body but also the soul.

Local Farms

Visiting a farm in Maui isn't just a tour; it's an immersion into the heart of the island's food culture. Places like O'o Farm in the misty uplands of Kula offer a glimpse into the journey from soil to plate. Here, you can pick your own salad greens, learn about the lifecycle of coffee, and enjoy a meal that's so fresh, it was growing around you just minutes before. It's an experience that connects you directly with the source of your food, grounding you in the reality of what it takes to bring each ingredient to your table.

Farm-to-Table Dining

Maui's restaurant scene is a vibrant showcase of the island's best produce, with chefs and restaurateurs passionate about sourcing locally. Dining at establishments like Merriman's Kapalua, where the menu changes with the seasons, reflects the island's bounty and the creativity it inspires in the kitchen. These meals celebrate Maui's agricultural heritage and are a testament to the flavors and traditions that define the island. They're not just delicious; they're stories of the land, served up on a plate.

Supporting Local

When you choose to dine farm-to-table in Maui, you're doing more than just enjoying a meal. You're supporting a network of local farmers, fishers, and artisans who are the backbone of the island's food culture. You're contributing to the local economy and helping to reduce the environmental impact of long-distance food transport. It's a simple choice with far-reaching effects, reinforcing the idea that good food is not just about taste; it's about community, sustainability, and respect for the land.

11.2 VOLUNTEERISM: GIVING BACK TO PARADISE

Maui, an island that captures the heart with its stunning landscapes and warm culture, thrives on the spirit of community and the shared responsibility to care for its natural and cultural treasures. For those who have experienced Maui's magic and wish to give back, numerous opportunities await to contribute time and energy to meaningful causes. Through volunteerism, visitors can immerse themselves in the island's ethos, creating a bond that transcends the typical tourist experience.

Volunteer Opportunities

Maui brims with projects aimed at conservation, restoration, and community enhancement. These initiatives welcome hands eager to make a difference, offering a range of activities to suit diverse interests and abilities:

- **Reef Preservation**: Join efforts to protect Maui's coral reefs by participating in underwater cleanups or coral restoration workshops. Organizations like the Maui Ocean Center offer programs where divers and snorkelers can learn about reef conservation while actively removing debris.
- **Forest Restoration**: Volunteers can help restore Maui's native forests. Projects often involve planting native species, removing invasive plants, and learning about the island's unique ecosystems. The East Maui Watershed Partnership provides such opportunities, allowing volunteers to contribute to the health of vital watersheds.
- **Cultural Heritage Sites**: Assist in the preservation of historical and cultural sites across the island. From restoring ancient fishponds to maintaining the trails and gardens of sacred sites, volunteers help maintain the physical and spiritual connection to Maui's past.
- **Community Agriculture**: Support local agriculture by volunteering at community farms and gardens. These projects not only promote sustainable food sources but also strengthen the bonds within communities. Farms like Hāna Farms welcome volunteers to learn about tropical agriculture while helping with daily tasks.

Making a Difference

Stories of volunteers who have left a lasting impact on Maui's communities and landscapes are a testament to the power of giving back. Consider the tale of a group that spent weeks removing invasive species from a crucial watershed, whose efforts resulted in the return of native birds to the area. Or the story of an individual who, through volunteering at a local farm, helped establish a community program that provides fresh produce to needy families. These narratives underscore the significant, lasting changes that can arise from volunteerism, illustrating how even a short stint of dedicated effort can ripple through the community and environment.

Responsible Travel

In embracing volunteerism, visitors adopt a stance of responsible travel, actively contributing to preserving and enhancing the places they visit. This approach to travel mitigates tourism's impact and enriches the visitor's experience, offering meaningful connections and insights that go beyond the conventional. Travelers partake in a reciprocal relationship with Maui by choosing to volunteer, receiving the gift of its natural beauty and cultural richness while offering their time and energy in return.

11.3 COMMUNITY AND CELEBRATION: PARTICIPATING IN LOCAL EVENTS

The heart of Maui beats in its festivals and local events, where the island's culture comes alive in a celebration of music, dance, tradition, and the spirit of Aloha. Each festivity, from the shores of Kapalua to the slopes of Haleakalā, invites residents and visitors to share in the joy and heritage that make Maui truly special. These gatherings are not just occasions but the island's lifeblood, painting each season with the colors of community and belonging.

Cultural Festivals

Maui's calendar is dotted with events that echo the island's diverse cultural landscape. The Maui Whale Festival celebrates the island's deep connection with the ocean giants, featuring parades, educational talks, and whale-watching tours. For a taste of local flavors, the Maui Onion Festival pays homage to the island's agricultural roots, with cooking demonstrations, food tastings, and live entertainment. The spirit of aloha is perhaps best experienced during the Aloha Festivals, where the richness of Hawaiian culture is on full display through music, hula, crafts, and a royal parade. Each event, big or small, is an invitation to dive deep into the heart of Maui's traditions and to celebrate the island's enduring spirit.

Luau

The luau holds deep historical and cultural significance in Maui and throughout Hawaii, serving as a traditional Hawaiian feast that symbolizes community, celebration, and hospitality. Historically, the luau marked important occasions such as victories in battle, royal birthdays, or successful harvests, bringing people together in a spirit of 'ohana (family) and aloha (love). It was a revolutionary event when King Kamehameha II removed the kapu (taboo) system, allowing men and women to eat together, transforming the luau into a symbol of unity and equality. Today, luaus celebrate Hawaiian heritage, featuring traditional foods like kalua pig, poi, and poke, alongside hula dancing and Hawaiian music, preserving and sharing the rich cultural traditions and history of the Hawaiian people with residents and visitors alike.

Event Highlights

While each festival offers its own unique charm, certain performances and ceremonies stand out, offering unforgettable glimpses into Maui's cultural heart. The hula, Hawaii's ancient dance, tells stories of the land, sea, and gods, with every movement rich in meaning. Witnessing a live hula performance, especially during competitions or cultural festivals, is a mesmerizing experience. Another highlight is the oli, or Hawaiian chant, an oral tradition that connects the present with the ancestors, the 'aina (land), and the spiritual world. Participating in a lū'au, where traditional foods are shared, and stories and dances are performed under the stars, offers another layer of connection to the island's heritage. These moments, among many others, are not just entertaining; they're doorways into the soul of Maui, inviting all who enter to experience the depth and beauty of its traditions.

11.4 THE KANIKAPILA: MUSIC AS A WAY OF LIFE

Music in Hawaii is more than just a form of entertainment—it's a lifeline to the past, a voice for untold stories, and a melodious thread weaving through the fabric of everyday life. It's in the air you breathe, the rhythm of the waves, and the rustle of palm leaves. This island's rich and deeply rooted musical heritage serves as a bridge between generations, carrying the legacy of its people and the spirit of the land.

Musical Roots

The origins of Hawaiian music trace back to the chants and rhythms of the early Polynesians, who used music as a means to record their history, celebrate their victories and honor their gods. These chants, or mele, laid the foundation for what would evolve into a unique musical tradition, deeply intertwined with the Hawaiian language and the natural cadences of the islands. Music became a vessel for Hawaii's soul, encapsulating its people's joys, sorrows, and everyday life.

Kanikapila Culture

Kanikapila, which translates to "let's play music," embodies Hawaiian music-making's communal and improvisational nature. Picture a group of friends gathering on the beach as the sun sets, each bringing an instrument or simply their voice, ready to share the joy of music. There's no set list, no rehearsals—just a spontaneous flow of melodies and rhythms that everyone, from toddlers to elders, can join in. This tradition highlights the inclusivity and communal spirit of the Hawaiian people, where music is a shared journey, and everyone is welcome.

Instruments of Aloha

At the heart of kanikapila are the instruments that carry the islands' voices. The 'ukulele, with its cheerful strumming, is perhaps the most iconic, its origins blending Portuguese influence with Hawaiian craftsmanship. Then there's the slack-key guitar, a style unique to Hawaii, where the strings are loosened, or "slacked," to produce a resonant, harmonious sound that echoes the laid-back pace of island life. The nose flute, or 'ohe hano ihu, and the ipu, a gourd drum, add to the ensemble, each contributing their distinct sounds to the symphony of kanikapila.

Experience Kanikapila

For visitors, the chance to dive into the kanikapila experience is a rare opportunity to connect profoundly with the island's culture. Beach parks often become impromptu stages for these musical gatherings, especially as the weekend draws near. Local bars and restaurants, too, host kanikapila nights, where musicians and patrons share in music creation. For those eager to participate, learning a few basic 'ukulele chords or simply lending your voice can be your ticket into the circle. In these moments, surrounded by laughter and song, the true essence of Maui reveals itself.

Through music, Maui's soul speaks. It tells of ancient legends and modern tales, love for the land and the deep connections that bind its people. Kanikapila, with its open invitation to all, reflects the spirit of Aloha—of sharing, inclusion, and community. Music has the timeless power to bring people together, creating moments of joy and unity that resonate long after the last note fades into the night.

MOUNTAIN MAGIC

12.1 UPCOUNTRY SERENITY: THE ROLLING HILLS OF KULA

Nestled on the slopes of Haleakalā, Kula greets you with open arms, its landscape a patchwork of farms and gardens that seem to stretch endlessly under the Maui sun. This area, known as the heartland of Maui's agriculture, thrives due to a unique microclimate that blankets the land in a gentle warmth by day and a refreshing coolness as dusk falls. It's a place where the earth is rich and the air is clear, inviting anyone with a love for the land to explore its bounty.

In Kula, the relationship between people and the soil is evident in every farm and field, where dedication to sustainable practices ensures that the land continues to give generously. Here, the famous Maui onions grow, their sweetness a result of the nurturing touch of Kula's farmers. Lavender farms dot the landscape too, painting the green with hues of purple and filling the air with a calming fragrance. These farms aren't just places of production; they're havens where the connection to the land is celebrated.

For those curious about the journey from seed to table, Kula offers an abundance of farm tours, each an opportunity to immerse in the agricultural life of Upcountry Maui. These tours are more than educational; they're sensory experiences. Walking through fields of lavender, the aroma enveloping you as bees buzz lazily from flower to flower. These tours provide insight into the farming techniques that make Maui's agriculture so unique, from organic practices to innovative water conservation methods.

- **Ali'i Kula Lavender Farm**: Here, visitors can wander through lavender gardens, participate in crafting workshops, and learn about the farm's sustainable practices.
- **Kula Country Farms**: Famous for its strawberries, this family-owned farm offers a hands-on experience with its pick-your-own-strawberries activity, a favorite among families.
- **Ocean Vodka Organic Farm and Distillery**: This tour offers a look into the production of organic spirits, from the farming of sugar cane to the distillation process, all with stunning ocean views as a backdrop.

But Kula's allure isn't just in its farmlands; it's also in the vistas that span across Maui and out to the ocean. The rolling hills of Upcountry provide a vantage point like no other, where the blues of the sky and sea merge on the horizon, and the contours of the island lay sprawled beneath you. It's a place for reflection, where the vastness of the view puts everything into perspective, reminding you of the sheer beauty of existence. Picnicking at a spot with such panoramic views, you can't help but feel a deep sense of gratitude for the moment, for the beauty that surrounds you, and for the island that shares its treasures so freely.

The essence of Kula, however, lies not just in its landscapes and produce but in the lifestyle and traditions of Upcountry Maui. Life here moves at a gentler pace, where community ties are strong and the connection to the land runs deep. Traditions are cherished, from the art of Hawaiian quilting, passed down through generations, to the annual festivals that bring the community together to celebrate the harvest, the arts, and the island's rich cultural heritage.

- **Kula's Living Room Conversations**: Locals often gather in cozy living rooms, sharing stories and music, an intimate way to experience the island's culture.
- **The Upcountry Farmers Market**: A weekly event where the community comes together to share the bounty of the land, from fresh produce to artisanal goods, offering a taste of the local lifestyle.

In Kula, every path leads to discovery, every farm tells a story, and every view inspires wonder. It's a place that invites you to slow down, to breathe in the cool, fragrant air, and to open your heart to the serenity that envelops this Upcountry haven. Here, amidst the rolling hills, you're reminded of the simple joys—of sun-warmed soil, of a meal shared with friends, of a landscape that stretches out in a promise of endless possibilities. It's a reminder that, sometimes, the most profound connections are made not in grand gestures, but in the quiet moments.

12.2 STARLIGHT SOJOURNS: STARGAZING ATOP HALEAKALA

High above the sleeping land and ocean, where the air is thin and the heavens sprawl out in a vast array of twinkling lights, Haleakala stands as a sentinel to the stars. Here, atop this ancient shield volcano, you find yourself closer not just to the stars, but to the stories they've been telling since time immemorial. The night sky, unpolluted by city lights, offers a clarity and depth that turns stargazing into a spiritual experience.

Celestial Wonders

Gazing up from the summit of Haleakala, the universe opens in a display of celestial splendor that few places on Earth can rival. You're not just looking at stars; you're witnessing galaxies, nebulae, and planets in a live show that's been running since the dawn of time. Shooting stars streak across the sky, each one a silent wish speeding through the darkness. Constellations, those ancient patterns that have guided travelers and inspired myths, are vivid and clear, from Orion's Belt to the Big Dipper. On certain nights, you might catch the ethereal glow of the Milky Way as it arches across the sky, a reminder of our place in this vast cosmic miracle.

Astronomical Significance

Haleakala isn't just a prime spot for casual stargazers; it's a hub for astronomical research, home to some of the world's most advanced observatories. These facilities, perched at the volcano's summit, take advantage of the clear skies and minimal light pollution to peer deep into the universe, unlocking secrets about everything from black holes to the birth of stars. For those who gaze up from the slopes below, it's comforting to know that, atop the same mountain, scientists are exploring the frontiers of our understanding, bridging the gap between the mysteries of the cosmos and our quest for knowledge.

- **Haleakala Observatories**: A cluster of research facilities that includes the Advanced Technology Solar Telescope, which studies the sun, and the Pan-STARRS Observatory, known for its work in detecting near-Earth objects and studying distant galaxies.

Stargazing Tips

A little preparation goes a long way to make the most of your night under Haleakala's stars. The summit's elevation means temperatures can drop significantly after sunset, so dressing in layers is a must. A thermos of hot tea or cocoa can ward off the chill, making your stargazing session a cozy affair. A red flashlight will help you navigate in the dark without disrupting your night vision, ensuring the stars remain the night's brightest lights.

- **Timing is Everything**: While the stars are always above, certain astronomical events, like meteor showers or planetary alignments, offer a special treat. Checking a stargazing calendar can help you plan your visit around these cosmic spectacles.
- **Let Your Eyes Adjust**: Give your eyes time to adapt to the darkness. This adjustment period, usually about 20 minutes, allows you to see more stars and makes the experience even more awe-inspiring.
- **Bring Binoculars or a Telescope**: While the naked eye can see plenty, a pair of binoculars or a small telescope can bring the heavens closer, revealing the moon's craters or Saturn's rings.

Mythology and Legends

The stars above Haleakala are not just points of light; they are characters in the stories and legends that weave through Hawaiian culture. These tales, passed down through generations, offer a glimpse into how the ancient Hawaiians understood and related to the cosmos. The constellation of Maui's Fishhook, known elsewhere as Scorpius, tells of the demigod Maui and his attempt to unite the islands. The Pleiades, or Makali'i, signal the start of the wet season and the Hawaiian New Year. Stargazing here becomes a journey through these myths, a way to connect with the island's heritage and understand how the stars have guided and inspired its people for centuries.

- **Navigational Stars**: The Polynesians, skilled navigators, used the stars to voyage across the Pacific. Learning about these navigational stars adds another layer to your stargazing, linking you to the voyagers who, long ago, navigated these same waters guided by the night sky.

On Haleakala's summit, as the stars wheel overhead in their silent splendor, you stand at the crossroads of science and myth, of the vastness of the universe and the depth of human wonder. It's a place where the night sky tells not just the story of the cosmos but also of Maui itself, a reminder of our enduring fascination with the stars and the stories they tell. Here, under the dome of the night, you're not just observing; you're partaking in a tradition as old as humanity itself—the simple act of looking up and wondering.

TALES OF THE UNEXPECTED

There's something about the first morning light in Maui that feels different. This island has a way of folding you into its narrative, making every encounter a story, every moment a memory. In the heart of the Pacific, the spirit of Aloha thrives not just as a greeting but as a way of life—a beacon for kindness, connection, and cultural richness.

13.1 ENCOUNTERS WITH ALOHA: STORIES OF KINDNESS

Heartwarming Hospitality

Visualize strolling down a sun-kissed beach, the salty air tangling your hair, when a local child, seeing your fascination with shell collecting, shares a rare find from their own collection. This simple act, rooted in the Aloha spirit, transforms a casual walk into a cherished memory. It's these moments of unexpected warmth and generosity from Maui's residents that paint the true picture of island hospitality. From waitstaff at eateries who remember your name to the local artist who takes the time to explain the story behind each creation, Maui wraps you in a blanket of kindness that feels like coming home.

The Ripple Effect

The kindness experienced in Maui doesn't end with your flight home. It starts a ripple effect, inspiring you to carry the Aloha spirit with you. You find yourself smiling at strangers more often, engaging in small acts of kindness, and sharing the stories of warmth and welcome you encountered. This spirit, once experienced, becomes a part of you, influencing your interactions and outlook. It's a testament to the island's power to touch hearts and change lives, not through grand gestures but through genuine, human connections.

13.2 MIRACLES IN MAUI: WHEN THE ISLAND HEALS

Maui's natural splendor has embraced countless visitors, who have found a sanctuary for healing. The island's landscapes, rich with life and bursting with the energy of creation, offer more than just scenic vistas; they provide a setting where the weary can find rest and the troubled can seek solace. Stories abound, each unique in detail but universal in theme: Maui has a profound capacity to heal.

Healing Journeys

Across the island, from the sun-drenched shores to the whispering bamboo forests, individuals recount transformative experiences. One visitor speaks of long walks along the Kapalua Coastal Trail, where the rhythmic sound of waves crashing against the rocks became a meditation, helping them process grief. Another describes a solitary hike through the dense bamboo forest on the Pipiwai Trail, where the stillness and the play of light through the stalks offered clarity and peace during a period of personal turmoil. In these stories, a common thread emerges: Maui, with its natural beauty and tranquil spaces, provides a backdrop against which individuals can confront their struggles, finding strength and renewal amidst its timeless landscapes.

Natural Therapies

The therapeutic properties of Maui's natural wonders are not merely anecdotal; they are grounded in the tangible benefits of spending time in nature. The island's beaches, renowned for their beauty, serve as natural therapy grounds where the simple act of walking barefoot in the sand can ground one's thoughts and soothe the soul. The forests, with their canopy of green and air rich with the scent of earth and plant life, act as natural lungs, offering visitors a chance to breathe deeply, releasing stress and absorbing the calm of the wilderness. By their very existence, these environments encourage mindfulness and presentness, essential components in the journey toward healing.

Spiritual Retreats

Maui is renowned for its diverse range of spiritual retreats and wellness programs, many of which incorporate the island's natural beauty and traditional Hawaiian healing modalities. Here are several retreats on Maui that offer unique experiences focused on wellness, healing, and spiritual growth:

1. **Heart Path Journeys**: Offers customizable retreats for individuals, couples, families, and small groups, focusing on personal growth, relationships, healing, spirituality, self-mastery, and wellness. The retreats are held in various locations across Maui, offering a combination of adventures, learning experiences, and growth opportunities.

2. **Hale Akua Garden Farm & Eco-Retreat**: Hosts a retreat called "Rebirth," which is a transformative holistic therapy, yoga, and healing retreat for grieving hearts. This retreat includes holistic therapies, group workshops, and one-on-one grief support, emphasizing deep healing and the transformative power of life.

3. **Maui Healing Retreat**: Offers customized holistic retreats for individuals focusing on restoring balance to the mind, body, and soul. The retreat utilizes various techniques such as yoga, with an experienced team of healers guiding participants on a personalized path to wellness.

4. **Lumeria Maui**: An educational retreat center located in Upcountry Maui, offering classes and programs in yoga, meditation, healing arts, metaphysical studies,

horticulture, Hawaiian culture, and dance & movement therapies. The property, originally built in 1910, has been renovated to support wellness and education.

5. **Maui Journeys**: Specializes in spiritual healing retreats and customized retreat journeys that embrace the Spirit of Aloha. These retreats are designed to offer a transformative experience, focusing on personal and spiritual growth.

Each of these retreats provides a unique opportunity to explore spiritual growth, healing, and wellness in the serene and uplifting environment of Maui. Whether you're interested in yoga, meditation, holistic therapy, or exploring Hawaiian culture and spirituality, there's a retreat on Maui that can cater to your interests and needs.

Connection to Nature

The profound impact of Maui's natural setting on healing and rejuvenation can be attributed to the deep connection it fosters with the natural world. This connection, instinctive yet often dormant, awakens in the presence of the island's vibrant life force. It reminds us that we are part of a larger ecosystem, subject to its rhythms and cycles. In recognizing this connection, visitors often find a sense of belonging and purpose, leading to significant emotional and spiritual growth. The majestic Haleakalā at sunrise, for instance, offers not just a visual spectacle but a moment of profound connection to the world's beauty and impermanence, a perspective that can shift attitudes and inspire change.

In Maui, miracles are not confined to the realm of the extraordinary. They unfold in the quiet moments of reflection by a tranquil shore, in the heartbeats shared with the island's natural rhythms, and in the journeys of healing and discovery that begin amidst its landscapes. These stories of transformation and renewal, told by those who have experienced Maui's restorative embrace, add to the island's legacy as a place where the spirit can find healing and where the heart can find peace.

13.3 LEGENDS ALIVE: MYTHS THAT SHAPE THE LAND

The Night Marchers: Encountering Hawaii's Ghostly Past

In the still of the night, when the moon casts its glow over Maui's landscapes, ancient tales stir in the shadows, bringing with them whispers of the past. Among these spectral stories, the legend of the Night Marchers stands apart, a haunting reminder of Hawaii's warrior history and the spiritual depth that permeates the island.

Phantom Processions

The Night Marchers, or Huaka'i Pō in Hawaiian, are said to be ghostly apparitions of ancient warriors, forever marching to the beat of distant drums. On certain nights, under specific lunar phases, they emerge, their torch-lit processions a mesmerizing sight to behold. These spirits are on an eternal march, visiting old battlefields, sacred sites, and areas significant to their once-earthly lives. Witnesses speak of a chill in the air as the marchers pass, their footsteps silent and their presence imposing, a spectral army locked in time.

Cultural Significance

The Night Marchers are deeply woven into Hawaiian folklore, embodying the profound respect and reverence for ancestors (kūpuna) that characterizes Hawaiian culture. Their appearances are not random; they are believed to be omens or messages from the past, reminding the living of the warriors' valor, the sacredness of the land, and the importance of maintaining a spiritual connection with one's heritage. The legends of the Night Marchers also serve as a bridge to understanding ancient Hawaiian society, its social structures, spiritual beliefs, and the valorization of warriors.

Respectful Awareness

For visitors intrigued by the possibility of encountering these spectral warriors, a respectful awareness is paramount. The legends come with protocols for those who find themselves in the path of the Night Marchers:

- **Avoidance**: If you hear drumming or see torches in the distance, it's wise to make yourself scarce. The Night Marchers are not to be disturbed.
- **Silence and Aversion**: Should you inadvertently find yourself near a procession, do not interrupt or attempt to communicate. Lower your gaze or lie flat on the ground in deference until they pass.

- **Sacred Spaces**: Many of the paths the Night Marchers tread are considered sacred. Understanding and respecting these sites' significance is crucial, whether or not you believe in the legends.

MEET THE NEIGHBORS

The Hawaiian archipelago, with Maui at its heart, is surrounded by a constellation of islands, each offering its own unique allure. From the bustling streets of O'ahu and the dramatic landscapes of Kauai to the tranquil shores of Lanai, the untouched Moloka'i, and the secretive Ni'ihau, these islands encapsulate Hawaii's diverse beauty and rich culture. Exploring these islands provides a deeper understanding of Hawaii's natural wonders, historical depth, and cultural vibrancy.

14.1 - O'AHU: THE GATHERING PLACE

O'ahu, known as "The Gathering Place," is the bustling center of the Hawaiian archipelago, where the energy of modern city life blends seamlessly with the tranquility of an island paradise. This island is home to Honolulu, the state's capital, and the famous Waikiki Beach, a hub for shopping, dining, and sun-soaked leisure. O'ahu offers a diverse array of experiences, from the solemn history of Pearl Harbor to the natural wonders of the North Shore's legendary surfing beaches.

Interesting facts about O'ahu include its role as a cultural melting pot, with influences from Asia, the Pacific, and the mainland USA creating a unique culinary and social atmosphere. The island's geography is just as diverse, featuring the iconic Diamond Head Crater near Waikiki, the lush Manoa Valley, and the dramatic cliffs of the Ko'olau Range.

For visitors, highlights include paying respects at the USS Arizona Memorial in Pearl Harbor, which commemorates the tragic events of December 7, 1941, and serves as a poignant reminder of the impacts of World War II. Adventure seekers can explore the North Shore, renowned for its massive winter waves and professional surfing competitions. Hiking Diamond Head offers panoramic views of the island, while a visit to the Polynesian Cultural Center provides insights into the rich heritage of the Pacific Islands.

O'ahu also boasts the Hanauma Bay Nature Preserve, a snorkeler's paradise with a spectacular coral reef ecosystem. The cultural heart of Honolulu pulses with life, offering arts, shopping, and dining experiences that showcase the island's multicultural heritage. With its blend of natural beauty, historical significance, and cultural richness, O'ahu stands as a microcosm of the Aloha spirit, inviting visitors to experience the depth and diversity of Hawaii.

14.2 - KAUAI: THE GARDEN ISLE

While living on Maui I found Kauai was a common destination for locals to 'go on vacation.' If you live on an island as magical as Maui and Kauai is your vacation destination, we must be talking next level fantasy land!

Kauai, known as "The Garden Isle," is the oldest and fourth largest of the Hawaiian Islands, celebrated for its lush landscapes, dramatic cliffs, and pristine beaches. This island paradise offers an escape into nature, with much of its territory inaccessible by road, preserving its beauty and tranquility.

One of the most captivating features of Kauai is the Na Pali Coast. With its towering sea cliffs, ancient valleys, and emerald hues, the Na Pali Coast epitomizes the untouched beauty of the island. Accessible only by foot, boat, or helicopter, it offers one of the most breathtaking vistas in Hawaii. Another natural wonder is Waimea Canyon, often referred to as the "Grand Canyon of the Pacific." Stretching 14 miles long and more than 3,600 feet deep, the canyon showcases a colorful array of rock layers, with hiking trails that afford spectacular views.

Kauai also boasts the Wailua River, the only navigable river in Hawaii, which leads to the enchanting Fern Grotto and Opaekaa Falls. The island's North Shore is home to the charming town of Hanalei and its iconic bay, offering stunning mountain backdrops and ideal conditions for surfing and paddleboarding.

Kauai makes frequent appearances in Hollywood films, from the classic "South Pacific" to "Jurassic Park," highlighting its picturesque and versatile landscapes. Kauai's commitment to preserving its natural environment and slow-paced lifestyle makes it a haven for those seeking to connect with nature.

For visitors, highlights beyond the Na Pali Coast and Waimea Canyon include snorkeling at Poipu Beach, exploring the botanical gardens of Limahuli and McBryde, and hiking the trails of Koke'e State Park. With its rich biodiversity, significant cultural sites, and breathtaking natural beauty, Kauai offers a serene and deeply rewarding Hawaiian experience.

14.3 LANAI: THE PINEAPPLE ISLAND

Lanai, often referred to as Hawaii's "Pineapple Island," offers a unique blend of luxury and rugged natural beauty, making it an exquisite retreat from the more tourist-centric islands. Once the world's largest pineapple plantation, Lanai has transformed into an island of extraordinary contrasts, with its luxury resorts and untouched landscapes.

For visitors, Lanai's highlights include the stunning landscapes of the Garden of the Gods (Keahiakawelo), a surreal and otherworldly desert area of rock formations that is best visited at sunset for its dramatic play of colors. Shipwreck Beach, on the north shore, offers intriguing views of a World War II-era shipwreck, with the backdrop of Molokai and Maui enhancing its scenic beauty.

The luxurious Four Seasons Resort Lanai provides world-class accommodations and access to the pristine Hulopoe Bay, a marine preserve with some of the best snorkeling spots on the island. For golf enthusiasts, the Jack Nicklausdesigned Manele Golf Course offers unparalleled ocean views on several holes.

Adventure seekers can explore Lanai's rugged backcountry by 4x4 tours, which navigate the island's diverse landscapes, from lunar terrains to lush forests. The Munro Trail, a challenging path, rewards hikers and off-road drivers with panoramic views of the archipelago.

Despite its size, Lanai is rich in experiences, offering a mix of luxury, adventure, and the opportunity to immerse oneself in the island's natural beauty and quietude. Its transformation from a pineapple plantation to a luxury retreat encapsulates the island's unique charm and appeal, making Lanai a must-visit destination within the Hawaiian Islands.

14.4 - MOLOKA'I: THE FRIENDLY ISLE

Moloka'i, often described as "The Friendly Isle," stands out in the Hawaiian archipelago for its deep-rooted connection to Native Hawaiian traditions and a markedly slower pace of life, offering a glimpse into Hawaii's past. Unlike its neighbors, Moloka'i has resisted the pull of commercial tourism, preserving its natural beauty and cultural heritage. This approach has allowed the island to maintain its rural charm and ensure that its landscapes, traditions, and community spirit remain largely untouched.

Reaching nearly 4000 feet, Moloka'i is home to the highest sea cliffs in the world, as recorded by the Guinness Book of World Records. These cliffs plunge dramatically into the deep blue waters of the Pacific Ocean. The island also houses Kalaupapa National Historical Park, accessible only by mule ride, hike, or small plane. This isolated peninsula was once a leper colony overseen by Father Damien, a figure of compassion and dedication to those suffering from Hansen's disease.

For visitors, Moloka'i offers unique experiences that highlight its natural beauty and cultural significance. The Papohaku Beach, one of the largest white sand beaches in Hawaii, provides a secluded spot for relaxation and contemplation. For those interested in outdoor adventures, the Halawa Valley offers breathtaking hikes through ancient landscapes, leading to majestic waterfalls and providing insights into the island's history and traditions.

Moloka'i's commitment to preserving its way of life extends to its agriculture, with local farms producing organic fruits and vegetables, contributing to the island's sustainability efforts. The Moloka'i Plumeria farm, where visitors can learn to make traditional Hawaiian lei, exemplifies the island's dedication to its cultural practices.

Embodying the essence of unspoiled Hawaii, Moloka'i invites visitors to step back in time. It offers a serene and profoundly authentic Hawaiian experience that contrasts sharply with the developed landscapes of its sister islands.

14.5 NI'IHAU: THE FORBIDDEN ISLE

Ni'ihau, known as "The Forbidden Isle," is the westernmost and seventh largest of the Hawaiian Islands. Its nickname stems from its private ownership by the Robinson family since 1864 and the strict limitations on outsiders visiting the island. This exclusivity has helped preserve its indigenous Hawaiian culture and natural environment, making Ni'ihau a fascinating subject of intrigue and mystique in the Hawaiian archipelago.

Unique to Ni'ihau is its commitment to maintaining the Hawaiian language as the primary language of its residents, making it one of the few places where Hawaiian is spoken fluently and daily. The island's isolation has preserved not only its language but also traditional customs and lifestyles, offering a living snapshot of Hawaiian culture before the influence of the outside world.

For visitors, access to Ni'ihau is highly restricted, with only a few options to experience its culture and natural beauty indirectly. Helicopter tours from Kauai offer aerial views of Ni'ihau's untouched landscapes, including its pristine beaches and the Lehua crater, a small, crescent-shaped islet off Ni'ihau's northern coast.

Ni'ihau is also famous for its exquisite shell leis, crafted from tiny, colorful shells found only on its shores. These leis are highly prized as cultural artifacts and are considered among the finest examples of traditional Hawaiian craftsmanship.

The island's combination of natural beauty, cultural preservation, and exclusivity has made Ni'ihau an object of fascination and respect. While visitors have limited direct experiences, Ni'ihau's allure lies in its role as a guardian of Hawaiian culture and natural splendor. It offers a poignant reminder of the archipelago's rich heritage and the importance of preserving it.

These islands, each with its distinct personality and offerings, surround Maui like jewels scattered across the Pacific Ocean. O'ahu pulses with energy and history, Kauai mesmerizes with its untouched natural beauty, Lanai offers secluded luxury, Moloka'i provides a window into traditional Hawaiian culture, and Ni'ihau guards its mysteries with quiet dignity. Visitors to these islands can look forward to a rich tapestry of experiences, from adventurous explorations and luxurious retreats to cultural immersions and historical discoveries, making their journey through Hawaii truly unforgettable.

MAUI TOMORROW: VISIONS OF THE FUTURE

Environmental Stewardship

The heart of Maui's future lies in its commitment to environmental stewardship. This commitment is visible in efforts to protect the island's unique ecosystems, from coral reefs to cloud forests. Marine sanctuaries are expanding, safeguarding the diverse underwater life that calls Maui's waters home. On land, reforestation projects are bringing native species back to life, restoring habitats and strengthening the island's biodiversity.

- **Community Clean-ups**: Regular beach and forest clean-ups, organized by local groups and supported by businesses and volunteers, have become a staple in Maui's environmental protection efforts. These efforts not only keep the landscapes pristine but also foster a sense of community responsibility towards the environment.

- **Sustainable Tourism Initiatives**: The tourism industry, a significant part of Maui's economy, is pivoting towards sustainability. Eco-friendly accommodations and tours are becoming the norm, and visitors are encouraged to participate in activities that contribute positively to the island's ecological health.

Cultural Revival

Maui stands at the forefront of a cultural revival, a renaissance of Hawaiian traditions, language, and arts that breathe life into the island's future. Schools dedicated to the Hawaiian language and cultural studies are thriving, nurturing a new generation fluent in the language of their ancestors and steeped in their traditions. Cultural festivals celebrate the rich heritage of the Hawaiian people, from music and dance to crafts and cuisine, inviting everyone to partake in the celebration of Maui's identity.

- **Hula Halau**: Hula schools, or halau, are at the heart of this revival, teaching not just the dance but the stories, chants, and philosophies that accompany it. These schools are vital in passing down traditional knowledge and keeping the spirit of aloha alive.
- **Cultural Workshops**: Workshops on traditional navigation, taro farming, and lei making offer hands-on experiences in Hawaiian culture. They provide both residents and visitors with a deeper understanding of the island's heritage and its relevance in today's world.

Future Challenges

Yet, as Maui looks to the future, it faces a delicate balance between growth and preservation. Development pressures threaten the very landscapes and ecosystems the community strives to protect. Climate change looms as a challenge, with rising sea levels and changing weather patterns posing a threat to Maui's natural beauty and biodiversity.

- **Community-Led Solutions**: In response, Maui's community is banding together, advocating for responsible development that honors the island's environmental limits and cultural significance. Local organizations are at the forefront of climate adaptation strategies, from coastal protection efforts to water conservation programs.
- **Education and Awareness**: Increasing awareness about the challenges facing Maui is crucial. Educational campaigns, community forums, and collaboration with scientists and environmental experts are fostering a well-informed community ready to tackle these challenges head-on.

In a world of constant change, Maui's vision for the future stands as a beacon of hope and innovation. It cherishes the island's natural treasures and cultural heritage and embraces the promise of a sustainable and vibrant future. Through collaboration, creativity, and a deep-rooted respect for the land and its people, Maui is navigating its path forward, ready to meet tomorrow's challenges while holding fast to the values that have shaped its past.

The Voyage Home: Taking Maui with You

When you first set foot on Maui, the island welcomes you with open arms, inviting you into a world where the essence of nature and the warmth of its people envelop you, leaving a mark that stays with you long after you've left its shores. It's in the way the sunsets paint the sky, the gentle lull of the ocean waves, and the spirit of Aloha that seems to permeate every interaction. Maui does more than just capture your heart; it transforms you, instilling a sense of responsibility and connection that transcends geographical boundaries.

Lasting Impressions

From the majestic peaks of Haleakalā to the serene waters of ʻĪao Valley, Maui imprints memories that linger, urging you to pause and appreciate the beauty around you. In these moments of reflection, you realize Maui is not just a destination; it's a feeling, a state of being that encourages you to live fully, with an appreciation for the natural world and empathy towards others. The island's landscapes are a vivid reminder of the earth's splendor, urging you to protect and cherish it wherever you roam.

Aloha Spirit

The essence of Aloha, with its foundations in love, kindness, and mutual respect, offers a blueprint for living that can transform communities. To carry the Aloha Spirit with you, approach life with a heart open to understanding, a willingness to help, and a commitment to bringing positivity into the lives of those you encounter. It's about moving through the world with a purpose, fostering connections that bridge divides, and creating ripples of kindness that can grow into waves of change.

- **Acts of Kindness**: Small gestures can have a profound impact, from sharing a meal to lending a listening ear. Make an effort to extend kindness, mirroring the hospitality experienced in Maui.
- **Community Engagement**: Get involved in local initiatives that aim to uplift and unite. Whether volunteering at a food bank or participating in a neighborhood clean-up, every effort counts.

Continuing the Connection

Maintaining a connection to Maui from afar means nurturing the values and experiences the island has instilled in you. It's about seeking ways to integrate the lessons learned into daily life, ensuring the island's spirit continues to inspire and guide you.

- **Cultural Appreciation**: Engage with Hawaiian culture through music, art, and literature. Support Hawaiian artists and creators by purchasing their work and participating in cultural events celebrating Hawaiian heritage.
- **Plan for a Return**: Keep the spirit of discovery alive by planning your next visit to Maui. Stay informed about the island's conservation efforts and look for ways to contribute, whether through donations or volunteer work during your stay.

In carrying Maui with you, you become an ambassador for the values the island represents, playing a crucial role in spreading the Aloha Spirit and advocating for a sustainable future. It's a nod to the transformative power of travel, where the journey doesn't end at departure but continues to shape us, urging us to live with intention and purpose.

As we move forward, let's hold onto Maui's essence, allowing it to guide our actions and interactions. In doing so, we carry a piece of the island with us, a constant reminder of the world's beauty and our responsibility to protect and preserve it for generations to come.

CONCLUSION

Here we are at the end of our Maui tour of natural wonders —a journey through its heart-thumping waterfalls, soul-soothing beaches, and moments when the Aloha Spirit didn't just touch our hearts but gave them a full-on bear hug. If you've made it this far, I'm guessing you're either really into Maui or you've developed a tolerance for my attempts at humor. Either way, I'm grateful.

Maui isn't just another tick on the ol' bucket list. It's a world of unmatched beauty, teeming with life both above and below the water, and bursting at the seams with cultures as vibrant as they are ancient. From the silent majesty of Haleakalā to the lively chirps in the Iao Valley, Maui is Mother Nature's canvas, painted boldly and with love. But what truly sets Maui apart isn't just the jaw-dropping land-scapes or the rich biodiversity; it's the people and their unwavering commitment to the Aloha Spirit. This isn't just a way of life; it's the lifeblood of the island, teaching us all a thing or two about kindness, compassion, and that sweet, sweet mutual respect.

Now, I'm not saying a trip to Maui will turn you into a new person, but I'm not not saying it either. There's something about the air here (and no, it's not just the humidity) that invites personal transformation. Whether it's a newfound respect for nature, a deeper connection with yourself, or a sudden urge to take up ukulele lessons, Maui leaves its mark on your soul.

And let's not forget the Herculean efforts to keep Maui's magic alive. Conservation isn't just a buzzword here; it's a rallying cry. From the depths where the humpbacks sing to the peaks kissed by the clouds, protecting Maui's natural and cultural treasures is a task we all share. Remember, every choice we make as travelers casts a stone across the waters of the future. Opting for that eco-friendly bungalow or joining a beach clean-up might seem small, but together, these ripples create waves.

So, what's the game plan? Simple: travel sustainably, tread lightly, and give back more than you take. Embrace Maui not just as a place to snap that perfect Instagram shot (though, let's be real, you'll get plenty of those), but as a living, breathing entity that welcomes you with open arms and an open heart.

Of course, Maui is always on the move, changing with the tides and the times. The island you'll meet is alive, teeming with stories waiting to be told and adventures waiting to be had. And when you do cross paths with its wonders, share those tales. Let your experiences inspire a legion of mindful travelers ready to experience the magic for themselves.

Finally, a big mahalo to you, dear reader, for embarking on this journey with me. Whether Maui is calling your name for the first time or welcoming you back like an old friend, I hope this book helps you navigate its wonders with an open heart and an eager spirit. Here's to the journey ahead – may it be filled with discovery, connection, and a whole lot of Aloha.

Safe travels, fellow wanderer. Maui awaits.

AFTERWARD: A KONA LOW

(The following tale is again a true story with made-up names for some reason).

It was the beginning of what was destined to be a long, long day...

Though 72 degrees and mild, the tropical breeze would soon build into a perpetual 10-day rain-buffeting gale known in these parts as a Kona Low. These particular weather events are infrequent, but when they do set in, you are in for a long, damp, windy bummer of a week in what was supposed to be a tropical paradise.

Many days, one might think my position as a Naturalist on the Pacific Whale Foundation's Ocean Voyager was the quintessential career choice for clean-livin'. Once, while 'lifeguarding' off Lanai (which mostly means floating in a kayak watching humpback whales frolic in the background while snorkelers flail in the foreground) I was accused of living 'the life of Reilly.'. Clearly, I was in no position to refute this.

Then there's working on a boat with 120 passengers when a Kona Low blows into the neighborhood...

If you run a whale-watching company on Maui, ' a Kona Low' is a phrase that will cause your face to scowl and your soul to shudder. Luckily, that particularly dreaded weather phenomenon generally only occurs once every few years.

Sadly for this season, however, the second such storm of the year was setting in at the beginning of the second busiest tourist week of the winter (the first storm wiped out the week over Christmas).

If there is ever a tragic sight, it is that of a father sitting on a bench in a mall on Maui (because that is the only indoor activity when there is a semi-hurricane going on outside). He is staring hopelessly at his wife and children who are staring back with their arms in the air wondering what they are supposed to be doing, bored out of their minds while a sideways rain has prevented them from ever stepping foot on the beaches they have dreamt of for months...the father with a look of exasperation and depression as the $25k he dropped on this trip will leave nothing but emotional scars...

The latest crop of tourists settling onto the island for their week of anticipated bliss probably had no idea what meteorological misery lay ahead. At the very least they clung to false hope. The folks lined up for our first of three whale watches of the day still wore smiles of anticipation somehow...

All of the crew on the Voyager knew their happy faces would fade after two long hours on cold, rough seas. Due to the inevitable tourist discomfort, we probably should not have been running tours that day. But we decided to push our luck and scrape out what earnings we could, knowing there most certainly wouldn't be any more boats leaving the harbor for the next nine or ten days.

Among the first batch of passengers we met while passing out Purser Maggie's breakfast muffins was a young couple from Chicago named Tessa and Jackson. The ridiculously incessant nature of their grins could only mean one thing...newlyweds or soon-to-be. It was confirmed after a short chat my crewmate Lindsay and I had with them that they were indeed to be married later that day. When we asked where and when we both reacted with the same subtle outburst of sorrow for their doomed plans...they promptly reacted with defiant glee and almost an inconceivable added excitement for the horrific conditions they would be destined to encounter later that day...

"We don't care if it's pouring rain and 100 mph winds, we will be standing on Makena Beach at exactly 5pm getting married" gushed the groom, 'And this will be the happiest day of our lives!' Tessa radiated joy beside him.

Lindsay and I admired their eternally positive attitude and wished them the best, knowing full well that their worst-case scenario for wedding weather conditions was imminent. I hope their wedding guests are able to absorb some of Tessa and Jackson's overwhelming optimism because Makena Beach was guaranteed to be a stormy nightmare by 5pm.

Sand will have blown into various nooks of their bodies, which they would then carry for life.

* * *

The first trip of the day went reasonably well. Despite the rough seas, only four of the sixty passengers spent much of the trip hanging over the railing, donating their partially digested breakfast muffins to the wee fishies. Some of the passengers were even still smiling as they disembarked, including the prospective newlyweds from Chicago.

As expected, conditions deteriorated for the next trip. The lineup on the railing grew and happy faces became few and far between.

By the time the third trip was due to begin, the notion of taking a herd of mainlanders out to sea for two hours was bordering on ludicrous. The driving sideways rain had begun, and yet there was a line of some 50-odd folks standing on the dock waiting for their dream boat ride!? Rather than the usual giddy anticipation, this group seemed to have a better understanding of what lay ahead and wore expressions closer to dread than excitement.

While everyone survived, it is more than likely that many of those folks have repeatedly since told the tale of the worst two-hour boat ride of their lives, which happened to be during their 'dream' Maui vacation. If any of them dared to open their eyes to catch a glimpse of the view during those two hours, they are likely still feeling the sting of saltwater embedded in their eyeballs.

I'll spare the details of the scene at the railing on this trip...

Not sure if any of you have suffered seasickness, but being trapped on a boat on a boiling sea with a freezing driving rain while vomiting incessantly makes for an experience more miserable than words can do justice to. These folks have no idea of the hatred they are capable of, towards people they didn't even know earlier that day. But that hatred is burning in their eyes as they disembark as we attempt to hold out the 'mahalo jar' in their general direction... Probably we should skip the tip jar routine on future trips of that nature...

Now that the last of the miserable folk is back on stable ground, the crew wants nothing more than to collapse into a pile of goo. Sadly, soooo sadly, there is still work to do, and it involves the back-breaking scrubbing of decks, which I'm most certain was never part of that Reilly fellow's life routine.

It wouldn't seem such an ominous task given we only serve pretzels on the afternoon whale watches. However, there is the added exhaustion this day brought, plus the little-known fact that when a ground-up pretzel is exposed to salt water and stepped on, it turns into a military-grade cement-type adhesive on the deck. It takes all of an able body's might to remove these in the best of times. But these were not the best of times, my friends. We all suffered from a delirium so intense Lindsay could have sneezed out a ginormous glob of snot, had it stuck and dangling three inches from her chin, and there would not have been a shred of strength or desire to mention it or for her to do a damn thing about it.

And so, we scrubbed the deck, miserably and in silence, in the driving sideways freezing rain of a kona low.

There was nothing in my field of vision but the infuriatingly crustified pretzel bits below me when... something... changed. Somehow the gray deck paint changed color just a shade. And it seemed like the sound of the world somehow changed, and the feeling of the air on my skin was different... Clearly, I was about to faint or something. I couldn't tell what it was, but it caused me to slowly come to a stop, and then almost fear looking up.

In the past few minutes, I hadn't noticed that the wind and rain had inexplicably calmed... but something else suddenly felt profoundly different about the universe at this moment... When I mustered the courage to look up what I saw was not possible.

One could have interviewed every meteorologist in the hemisphere, and all would have said the same thing: what was happening was simply not possible. The cloud bank associated with this Kona Low is thousands of feet thick, and this formation was already extending literally hundreds of miles beyond the horizon in every direction. While it was highly improbable that the wind and rain had temporarily relented, it was truly impossible that the sun, right as it was reaching the sea, found a gap in the clouds.

This cloud bank was so dense and low that it was as if it was never meant to reflect the rays of the sun. No human or whale or turtle could have ever witnessed such an awesome sight. What ensued was a more intense, miraculous explosion of color than the most magical of imaginations could have dreamt. It was as if both the sea and sky were set afire with a soothingly warm, infinitely calming flame. A glance around to my crew mates saw nothing but humans frozen in a moment of hopeless bliss. Captain Mark with dropped jaw, Codi with fire orange reflective streaks streaming down her face...

Then something occurred to me that seemed to cause my heart to break the picture frame like the Grinch's once did. My knees almost gave out, but I caught myself. Standing near me, Lindsay noticed my expression turned to an even more astonished state and asked: "What?" I somehow knew what I was going to see even before I looked at my watch, and sure enough, it read exactly '5:00'.

I said nothing, but I looked at my watch with a motion of my eyes, then nodded my head off into the distance toward Makena Beach. Now there were five of us with fire orange streaks running down our faces.

We were all left entirely speechless for the remainder of the shift (aside from some sniffles and the normally stoic Captain Mark's weeping noises), but the glow that blazed from our eyes, in pure joyful defiance of our weary bodies, spoke for us all.

The impossibly warm, calm, brilliant sunset lasted for about an hour. Then the storm slowly set back in and did not relent for eight miserable days. I sincerely hope those newlyweds from Chicago found some way to keep a positive perspective and make the best of their time while trapped in their hotel room for the remainder of their Maui honeymoon...

REFERENCES

Lahaina Historic District https://www.nps.gov/places/lahaina-historic-district.htm

Lahaina's Historic Banyan Tree Is Scarred, but Standing https://www.nytimes.com/2023/08/10/us/lahaina-banyan-tree.html

Lahaina Galleries https://www.lahainagalleries.com/

Six Months After Lahaina Fire, Long Recovery Continues https://weather.com/news/weather/news/2024-02-08-lahaina-fire-six-months-housing-recovery

The Law of the Aloha Spirit https://www.hawaii.edu/uhwo/clear/home/lawaloha.html

Kapu (Hawaiian culture) https://en.wikipedia.org/wiki/Kapu_(Hawaiian_culture)

Volcano Watch — Maui Nui, the Bigger Island https://www.usgs.gov/news/volcano-watch-maui-nui-bigger-island

How Hawaiians Saved Their Language | Folklife Today https://blogs.loc.gov/folklife/2017/05/how-hawaiians-saved-their-language/

Haleakalā National Park https://www.conservationfund.org/projects/haleakala-national-parks

Maui Natural Area Reserves https://dlnr.hawaii.gov/ecosystems/nars/maui/

What Climate Change Means for Hawaii - US EPA https://19january2017snapshot.epa.gov/sites/production/files/2016-09/documents/climate-change-hi.pdf

Microclimates on Maui https://www.skylinehawaii.com/blog/mauis-microclimates

Humpback Whales in Maui | Whales Visit December To April https://hawaiianpaddlesports.com/maui/humpback-whales/

Manta Ray diving on Maui https://mauiundersea.com/manta-ray-diving-on-maui/

Coral Reefs | Mauka to Makai Restoration https://dlnr.hawaii.gov/coralreefs/mauka-to-makai-restoration/

Viewing Marine Wildlife in Hawaiʻi https://www.fisheries.noaa.gov/pacific-islands/marine-life-viewing-guidelines/viewing-marine-wildlife-hawaii

Maui Forest Bird Recovery Project – Put Extinction in the Past https://www.mauiforestbirds.org/

Native Hawaiian Plants: My Plant ID Guide — noahawaii https://noahlangphotography.com/blog/native-hawaiian-plant-guide

Haleakalā Silverswords https://www.nps.gov/hale/learn/nature/silversword.htm

Invasive species have created a cycle of wildfire in … https://grist.org/wildfires/invasive-species-have-created-a-cycle-of-wildfire-in-hawai%CA%BBi-can-maui-break-it/

Pīpīwai Trail & the Bamboo Forest: The Complete Hiking Guide https://www.earthtrekkers.com/pipiwai-trail-hike/

Hiking - Haleakalā National Park (U.S. … https://www.nps.gov/hale/planyourvisit/hiking.htm

12 Maui Waterfalls that will take your breath away (with a … https://boutiquehawaii.com/maui-waterfalls/

West Maui - Images of Old Hawaii https://imagesofoldhawaii.com/wp-content/uploads/West-Maui-Background-Summary.pdf

Ode to Lahaina - Surfer | Surf Stories https://www.surfer.com/surf-stories/ode-to-lahaina

The best kitesurfing spots in Maui, Hawaii - Kiterr.com https://kiterr.com/kitespots/north-america/best-kitesurfing-spots-maui-hawaii/

Green Initiatives - Extended Horizons | Dive Maui & Lanai https://extendedhorizons.com/green-initiatives/

Snorkeling At Night - See Unique Creatures But Be Prepared https://www.tropicalsnorkeling.com/snorkeling-at-night/

The Best 5 Farm-To-Table Restaurants on Maui https://www.hawaiimagazine.com/the-best-5-farm-to-table-restaurants-on-maui/

Volunteer Opportunities on Maui (Hawaii) - Conservation http://www.hear.org/volunteer/maui/index.html

Maui Events Calendar https://www.gohawaii.com/islands/maui/events

Kanikapila - Wikipedia https://en.wikipedia.org/wiki/Kanikapila

Iao Valley State Park https://www.gohawaii.com/islands/maui/regions/central-maui/iao-valley-state-park

Stargazing - Haleakalā National Park (U.S. … https://www.nps.gov/hale/planyourvisit/stargazing.htm

Farm Tours on Maui https://www.gohawaii.com/islands/maui/things-to-do/land-activities/farm-tours

PANIOLO CULTURE - Ulupalakua Ranch https://ulupalakuaranch.com/paniolo-culture/

What are heiau? - Manoa Heritage Center https://www.manoaheritagecenter. org/moolelo/kuka%CA%BBo%CA%BBo-heiau/what-are-heiau/

Iao Valley State Park's Cultural Significance https://www.hawaiistateparks. org/blog/iao-valley-state-parks-cultural-significance

Labyrinths https://sacredgardenmaui.com/labyrinths/

07/07/21-OLOWALU PETROGLYPHS DAMAGED IN ... https://dlnr.hawaii. gov/blog/2021/07/07/nr21-128/

Mālama 'Āina Service Projects 2022 http://www.mauihealth.org/blog/ posts/m%C4%81lama-%C4%81ina-service-projects-2022/

Hawaiian Islands Humpback Whale National Marine ... https://dlnr.hawaii.gov/ dar/marine-managed-areas/hawaiian-islands-humpback-whale-national-marine-sanctuary-hihwnms/

Coral Reefs | Mauka to Makai Restoration https://dlnr.hawaii.gov/coralreefs/ mauka-to-makai-restoration/

Maui scientists and nonprofits seek volunteers https://spectrumlocalnews.com/ hi/hawaii/community/2022/03/26/maui-scientists-and-nonprofits-seek-volunteers

Sustainable Tourism Association of Hawaii | Hawaii STAH ... https://www. sustainabletourismhawaii.org/

The Best 5 Farm-To-Table Restaurants on Maui https://www.hawaiimagazine. com/the-best-5-farm-to-table-restaurants-on-maui/

Leave No Trace - Hawai'i Volcanoes National Park (U.S. ... https://www.nps. gov/havo/planyourvisit/leavenotrace.htm

Sustainable Travel and Ecotourism in Maui https://www.frommers.com/desti nations/maui/planning-a-trip/sustainable-travel--ecotourism

The Aloha Spirit Law https://www.skylinehawaii.com/blog/the-aloha-spirit-law

Survival Stories from the Maui Wildfires https://www.outsideonline.com/ outdoor-adventure/environment/maui-fires-lahaina-relief-volunteer-effort/

The Incredible Myths and Legends of Hawaii https://www.fodors.com/world/ north-america/usa/hawaii/experiences/news/the-incredible-myths-and-legends-of-hawaii

Nightmarchers https://en.wikipedia.org/wiki/Nightmarchers

Lahaina Historic Trail – Where History & Culture Come Alive https:// historichawaii.org/2014/02/24/lahaina-historic-trail-where-history-culture-come-alive/

The Maui Fire Was Fueled by Centuries of Extractive Farming https://civileats. com/2023/08/23/how-two-centuries-of-extractive-agriculture-helped-set-the-stage-for-the-maui-fires/

Environmental Protection & Sustainability https://www.mauicounty.gov/742/Environmental-Protection-Sustainability

Hawaiian Renaissance - Wikipedia https://en.wikipedia.org/wiki/Hawaiian_Renaissance#:

Made in the USA
Monee, IL
18 December 2024